Understanding Eastern Europe

The Context of Change

Dr John M Howell
Senior East European Partner
of Ernst & Young

KOGAN
PAGE

First published in 1994

Kogan Page Limited
120 Pentonville Road
London N1 9JN

This book reflects the personal views of the author, John Howell, and are not necessarily those held by Ernst & Young.

British Library Cataloguing in Publication Data

A CIP record for this book is available from the British Library

ISBN 0 7494 1510 X

Typeset by Ernst & Young
Printed and bound in Great Britain by Biddles Ltd, Guildford and King's Lynn

DR JOHN M HOWELL

John Howell, Ernst & Young's Senior East European Partner, was described by The Times as an informed pundit on central and eastern Europe and by Accountancy Age as '... the most experienced of the Big 6 representatives (for central and eastern Europe)'. Widely regarded as an international guru on the region, he is an experienced and frequent broadcaster on events in the region for the BBC, CNN, Sky and FT-TV and a regular contributor to the press.

He is a member of the advisory board to the Know How Funds – the British Government's assistance programme to central and eastern Europe. He is also a member of the UK government advisory body – the East European Trade Council. He is a permanent member of the Kazakh-British Trade and Industry Council and of the British-Romania Trade Committee. He is currently chairman of British Invisibles' Central and East European Panel.

He initiated and led Ernst & Young's entry into the markets of central and eastern Europe, negotiating many of the joint ventures and co-operation agreements with local professional services firms on which the Ernst & Young network there was originally based. He has advised many leading companies on accessing these markets and has been involved in some of the major privatisation and financial infrastructure projects being undertaken there.

John was educated at the University of Edinburgh and St. John's College, Oxford and also with the Universities of Liverpool, Paris and Marie-Curie Sklodowska in Lublin, Poland.

Contents

		Page
Abbreviations		x
List of Tables		xii
List of Figures		xiii
Preface		xiv
1	**The End of an Era**	1
	The fall of the Berlin Wall	1
	The consequences of the fall	3
	A mixed picture of reform	5
	A poor western response	7
	The IMF	7
	A new world institution	10
2	**Progress to Reform: the Winners and Losers**	12
	Poland	14
	Czech Republic	17
	Hungary	20
	Slovenia	22
	Estonia	23
	Latvia	25
	Bulgaria	27
	Kazakhstan	29
	Russia	31
	Slovakia	34
	Belarus	36
	Lithuania	38
	Romania	39
	Croatia	41
	Uzbekistan	42
	Albania	44

Kyrgystan 46
Ukraine 48
Azerbaijan 50
Turkmenistan, Armenia, Tadzhikistan, Georgia, Moldova 52

3   The Transfer of Know How 55
Politics has not kept pace 57
A new Marshall Plan was rejected 59
How effective has the know-how transfer been? 60
Use of consultants has been naive 61
Project definition could be improved 63
Who benefits? 64
What is required and where are we now? 65
A level of co-ordination is required 68
The World Bank 68
Conclusions 69

4   The Return to the Private Sector 71
Why privatise? 71
What type of privatisation? 73
What are the objectives? 77
The emphasis of the various privatisation methods 78
The case of HungarHotels 81
The major problems 82
Post-privatisation success 82
Conclusions 85
Case studies 86

5   Rebuilding Local Industry 92
What is the basic underlying problem? 94
Reforming sectors 96
Reforming companies 100
Conclusions 103

Contents

6   How the 'West' Have Invested   106
How has the investment been made?   108
The expectations' gap   111
What are the capital requirements of central and
eastern Europe?   113
The contribution investors can make   114
Non-capital contributions   114
Why a lack of investment?   117
Competitive advantage   117
The principal inhibitors   120
The effect of government assistance   122
The impact of aid and assistance   124
Closing the expectations' gap   126
Case study   128
Portfolio investment   132
Conclusions   134

7   Culture and Attitudes   137
Cultural implications for business   148

8   Conclusions   153
Improved co-ordination is required   154
Less protectionism is required   155
Other expectations' gaps can be narrowed   157
New economic indicators are required   158
The positive aspects   160

Abbreviations

CIS The Commonwealth of Independent States: the organisation to which former Soviet republics belong

COMECON The Council for Mutual Economic Activity: the mechanism by which the USSR controlled the economies of central Europe

EBRD The European Bank for Reconstruction and Development: a world bank specialising in central and eastern Europe

EC The Commission of the European Union: the bureaucratic function of the EU

EEIM East European Investment Magazine: a US database

EFTA European Free Trade Area

EIU Economist Intelligence Unit

EU The European Union: the successor to the European Economic Community

GAZ Gorky Automobile Works: the makers of the Chaika Limousine

GDP Gross Domestic Product

G7 The Group of Seven leading industrialised nations

G24 The Group of Twenty-Four leading countries

IFC The International Finance Corporation: the private sector arm of the World Bank

IMF The International Monetary Fund: the institution charged with the task of maintaining world currency stability

KHF The Know How Fund: the assistance programme of the UK government for central and eastern Europe

MBO   Management buy-out

MIGA   Multinational Investment Guarantee Agency

NAFTA   North American Free Trade Agreement

OECD   Organisation for Economic Co-operation and Development

OPIC   Overseas Private Investment Corporation

PHARE   The EU's technical assistance programme for central and eastern Europe

TACIS   The EU's technical assistance programme for the former Soviet Union

USAID   The US Government's overseas aid and technical assistance programme

SAS   Scandinavian Airlines System: the jointly owned airline of the Scandinavian countries

UNDP   United Nations Development Programme

UNESCO   United Nations Educational, Scientific and Cultural Organisation

List of Tables

Page

2.1   Individual country ratings   13

3.1   Principal providers of technical assistance   56

4.1   Privatisation methods   73
4.2   Mass privatisation methods   75
4.3   Percentage of GDP originating in the private sector
      as at 31 December 1993   85

5.1   Percentage of western investors in favour of
      restructuring an existing company   93
5.2   Main performance indicators of Videoton   101
5.3   Key performance indicators of Tatra   103

6.1   Cumulative, committed foreign investments:
      1 January 1990 - 31 December 1993   106
6.2   Estimates of capital requirements in central and
      eastern Europe   113
6.3   Principal sectors of foreign investment in central and
      eastern Europe as at 31 December 1993   115
6.4   Average size of investments in central and
      eastern Europe as at 31 December 1993   119
6.5   Principal countries investing in central and
      eastern Europe as at 31 December 1993, by value   121
6.6   Assistance and investment ratios   125
6.7   OECD exports from central Europe   135

7.1   Changing attractiveness of countries   138

8.1   Aluminium imports from the CIS into the EU   156
8.2   CIS aluminium production costs as a percentage
      of western costs   156
8.3   Ownership of goods per 100 households   161

List of Figures

		Page
2.1	Actual foreign investment in Poland	14
2.2	Foreign investment in the Czech Republic	17
2.2a	Breakdown of foreign investment in the Czech Republic by Industry Sector	18
2.3	Actual numbers of foreign investments in Belarus	36
2.4	Actual numbers of foreign investors in Kyrgystan	46
3.1	The 'consultancy tourism' trap	63
3.2	Model of development	65
5.1	A process for better restructuring	105
6.1	Number of foreign investment enterprises	107
6.2	Methods for foreign investment	109-110
6.3	Stock Exchange values and weekly turnover	134
7.1	Main concerns of foreign investment in Poland	139
7.2	Telecommunications infrastructure	140
7.3	General infrastructure	140
7.4	Banking effectiveness	141
7.5	Legal environment	141
7.6	Access to various inputs	142
7.7	Countries for future investment	143
7.8	Are things generally proceeding in a right or a wrong direction in your country?	144
7.9	How contented or discontented are you with the progress of democracy?	144
7.10	Quality of life	145
7.11	Motivation	146
7.12	Managerial competence	146
7.13	Percentage opting for A rather than B	150
7.14	Percentage opting for testifying against a friend	151

Preface

I first went to eastern Europe for Ernst & Young in 1987, a visit occasioned by the introduction of the first foreign investment law in the then USSR since Lenin. I had previously been involved in the region since the late 1970s as an academic. In those days, the planes were small and uncomfortable but often empty. You knew with whom you were dealing in a rigid, if corrupt, hierarchy of seemingly infinite bureaucratic gradations. The poor standard of hotels was more than made up for by open camaraderie with your fellow travellers, of whom few were direct competitors anyway.

If that sounds like nostalgia for a more straight-forward time, it isn't. No one who visited eastern Europe at that time can surely forget the overwhelming intimidation on arrival and departure. An intimidation which, on one occasion at a check-point open to the winds, entailed a customs search through a large box of tissues – tissue by tissue – until they were all heaped on the passenger seat of the car.

Few who dipped below the surface of their immediate contract negotiations could have avoided being aware of the degrading political, social and economic conditions of the people and the futility of a system which was squandering economic and human resources for the sake of a bankrupt ideology.

But as western observers and participants in the dismantling of the old regime and in the process of reform, what motivated us to help? What ideologies, if any, could we offer to replace the seemingly discredited legacy of Marx and Lenin?

There is not a single answer to that question, of course. For some institutions the motivation was humanitarian aid. For others, a strong political motivation to sell capitalism (variously defined) was dominant. While for others still, it was a mixture of greed, genuine commercial interest, simple opportunism, etc.

Indeed, the failure of the west to be able to answer that question in the singular illustrates much of the problem in trying to evaluate the effectiveness of the contribution we have made to the reform process. There were no agreed objectives (other than those so superficial as to be banal) against which performance could be measured. There was no one ideology. There was no agreed concept of capitalism and there was a seemingly infinite variety of models of a market economy, most of which were paraded before the east Europeans as if in a shop window, except that it was a shop window from which the shop keeper not only offered his goods but also the money to pay for them, via one multilateral or bilateral aid programme or another. It was not a question of 'you pay your money and you take your choice'. You took your choice and then played one organisation off against another to minimise the strings attached to the money you were given to make the purchase in the first place.

The strict economic conditions imposed by institutions such as the IMF have not been part of the creed of the EU or EBRD. Few took a holistic view of social, economic and political reform as being necessarily interlinked and, just like western Europe post-1945, there was little in the way of detailed analysis of the problems or deep thinking about the potential answers.

It is only seven years since that 1987 visit. It is only five years since the Berlin Wall came down and fewer since the Czechoslovak Velvet Revolution. While much has changed rapidly, is it any more than superficial? Has the 'West' covered itself in credit in helping the reform process? Have the central and east Europeans grasped the opportunities before them? Has the foreign business community shown sufficient interest or vision? Is it all over now bar a few lingering pockets of reform (and, of course, the former Soviet Union)? Have world markets changed so rapidly in these five to seven years that central and eastern Europe is a dead story and a dead opportunity?

This book arose principally through frustration at trying to get an answer to these questions or even in trying to get a fuller picture from which an answer could be produced. It was born of frustration with the major lending institutions, for the growing irrelevance of their programmes and lack of effective co-ordination between them. It was born, too, of frustration with multi-nationals for which an immediate increase in earnings per share was usually more important than long-term thinking. It was born, too, of frustration with central and eastern Europeans and their nationalist pre-occupations which prevented long-term commercial opportunities being taken on a collective basis.

Preface

Frustration no doubt produces some odd books. In this case, I hope it has produced a book which has steered clear of an instant 'doing business in ...' format which would be rapidly out-of-date and has moved more to present my view of the underlying contexts, both eastern and western, in which the reform process is embedded and which are the inescapable environment now and for the future of central and eastern Europe.

It is based on my observation that while there are many changes occurring in the region, many have no immediate or deep impact on that environment or the underlying culture, and that our inability to understand that context will be seen as one of the biggest reasons for failure if the reform process falters.

One of the principal problems in producing a book on central and eastern Europe is the quality, quantity and timeliness of the relevant underlying data. Few statistics are prepared sufficiently quickly to be able to spot current changes in trends. These have more often to be gleaned from frequent visits, long conversations and the evidence of your own eyes in a wide range of different businesses.

Many statistics are produced on an inconsistent basis between countries making comparison hazardous. Many statistics have not been produced on a consistent basis from year to year in individual countries themselves. Statistics produced under the former central planning regimes were notoriously unreliable and even deliberately falsified.

As a result, there will be times when assertions made in this book can be backed up by nothing more than personal experience. In this respect I have been fortunate to be able to draw upon the intelligence gathered by Ernst & Young's extensive network of local offices in the region and the opinions of my fellow members on the Know How Fund Advisory Board, British Invisibles' Central European Panel and the other UK bodies on which I have served, such as the East European Trade Council.

In particular, I would like to thank EEIM, The World Economic Forum and EBRD for assistance with statistical data and Sally Croft and Gillian Parsons for their help in undertaking research. I would also like to thank Ewa Turowska and Kay Sullivan for their help in the production of the book.

The views, prejudices and errors remain my own.

1

The End of an Era

THE FALL OF THE BERLIN WALL

Every commentator on central and eastern Europe has begun their overview with the use of hyperbole to describe the changes which have occurred over the past nine years since Mikhail Gorbachev was elected General Secretary of the Communist Party of the USSR. Terms such as 'momentous', 'unprecedented' are regular epithets in the literature. This commentator is no exception. The changes *have* been unprecedented and momentous. A certainty in international political and economic life which lasted some forty-five years was effectively smashed overnight. That certainty was based on a bipolar world dominated by two superpowers – the USA and the USSR. While the most obvious signs of this confrontation could be found in Europe, such as the Berlin Wall, the 'cold war' which came with it was fought out in the third world. The momentous changes which have occurred in Europe, therefore, have been nothing to the changes which are occurring there. Even in South Africa, for example, other commentators have pointed to the speed with which apartheid was abandoned, once the threat of communism worldwide had diminished and the tacit support for South Africa as a bulwark against the spread of Soviet client states in Africa was no longer required.

Along with these changes came new pressures on existing world and regional institutions. These institutions were also, by and large, set up to deal with a bipolar world. Our expectations that they could satisfactorily cope with the new situation, even assuming the political will to do so, were probably intensely naive. Indeed, without the overriding focus of a stand against communism, many of the country members of these institutions quickly degenerated into naked self-interest. The emerging economic blocks exemplified by NAFTA, the EU, etc were not strong enough to replace the crusading, anti-communist zeal which had characterised the bipolar world and held it together. In many developed western economies these changes coincided with, and were part of, increasing internal instability, witnessed by a questioning of domestic certainties as to that country's role in the world and a questioning of, and cynicism towards, established institutions and social behaviour far deeper even than the youth rebellion of the 1960s.

Despite the appearance of uniformity across the Eastern Bloc, tensions could also be discerned there throughout the 1970s and 1980s as well. Although legendary, Polish antipathy to the USSR took increasingly overt forms. On one occasion in the late 1970s, for example, while camping on a student expedition along the Bug, the Poles insisted on setting up the site latrines on the Soviet side of a small island in the river simply to make a rather inconvenient political point!

Associated with such extreme behaviour was the continuity of indigenous cultures, often of great antiquity. In those parts of the region where literacy was weakest, such traditions were naturally passed on orally. But even in the most literate parts, the need to keep overt cultural manifestations to a minimum also acted to keep oral traditions alive. What power such traditions have, compared with the more anodyne literary word, in keeping alive not only the positive aspects of culture but also long-held prejudices and hatreds, which were later to emerge in Yugoslavia, for example!

At a national level, too, the 1970s and 1980s saw the beginnings of economic experiments in the Soviet satellite countries and a gradually closer relationship with western capitalism, including direct foreign investment in the form of joint ventures.

Increasingly, therefore, just as the West was doubting the philosophical basis on which our society rested, the Soviet Bloc lost even the willingness to pay lip-service to Marxism-Leninism. A more pragmatic view of economics emerged, less certain and without a 'noble' ideal attached to it.

When the Wall came down, therefore, neither camp was as uniform or as consistent as the stereotypes of the previous 45 years had led us to believe. Tensions were being exhibited by both sides and it was inevitable that one would influence the other. In this respect, of course, within a European setting the irony was that as one end of Europe reacted strongly against belonging to a supra-national organisation, the other end of Europe was moving closer to a federal European State. At one end of Europe, more and more power was being seized by an ever-increasing number of nation States, while at the other end of Europe national sovereignty was gradually being eroded in favour of a wider collective action. The interplay between these tensions and the influence of one on the other has yet fully to run its course. The early admission of the central European States to the EU may well significantly affect the move to political and economic union overall.

THE CONSEQUENCES OF THE FALL

One consequence of the changes which dramatically came to a head with the fall of the Wall was the increased globalisation of world markets. The introspective nature of COMECON and its formalised structure had meant that few independent channels of economic relationship were developed within the Bloc. Trade between the Bloc and the rest of the world was also run along formalised lines, with little direct participation by the Bloc in world economic development.

As the non-Soviet world, therefore, developed more and more complex layers of economic and political relationship in a dynamic but unpredictable way, the Bloc sank into stagnation and increasing indebtedness to foreign financial institutions. The borrowed funds never went into developing new export growth but into keeping the production-led, command economy alive, without western technology, access to which was restricted by the CoCOM committee. When that economy could not keep pace with demand even in basic essentials, general frustrations with politically-inspired limitations on freedoms and a disbelief in an overriding ideology made change inevitable. Suddenly, the edifice which had kept the Bloc out of world markets crumbled, and a major geographical area of the world suddenly became subject to the complex web of relationships which make up world markets.

Certainly, there was considerable naivety as to how world

markets worked, how capital was raised, why it was invested, etc, but many of these naive ideas can also still be found in the West. There was, in many quarters, a belief that world market capitalism had more rules and was more predictable in its operation than actually is the case. Notions of international competitive advantage were not understood. Foreign capital and foreign assistance were widely seen as the saving combination, although few were really prepared to pay the price of having the interference and participation of the fund providers in their internal affairs.

Yet despite these shortcomings, the Bloc was surely reasonable in expecting that the developed world would, and could, assist substantially in its change to market economies. After all, it had just witnessed the boom of the 1980s with increased affluence, increased world market activity and investment, profits, and a belief in the long term.

With impeccable timing, however, the Wall came down as this phase ended and the recessionary 1990s began. The emphasis switched to the short term, losses, low market activity, cautious investment policies and high interest rates. Talk of a Marshall Plan to rescue central and eastern Europe was quickly shot down as the cost of such a programme was calculated in direct terms, and in continued higher interest rates and prolonged recessions. Moreover, one key player virtually disappeared from the scene for a while, as Germany sank its resources, and swept in the resources of others, to achieve reunification.

For central and eastern Europe the juxtaposition of these factors with the overriding desire to abandon instantly the mechanism of COMECON meant inevitably a cataclysmic collapse in trade almost overnight and a scramble to re-orientate trade towards a protectionist EU. The adoption of world market prices and price and currency liberalisation were accompanied by a slump in overall economic activity throughout the area and the increasing spectacle, especially in the former USSR, of factories standing still and idle. Even where trade continued between former COMECON members, the banking system was inadequate to deal with direct trading at different levels between individual enterprises.

The suddenness of the abandonment of traditional markets in the former USSR was clearly dictated by political concerns. The issue of whether it would have been better to transform COMECON into two trading blocs – the former USSR and the rest – was never widely debated. Economic and political reality was unable to do more than create a Visegrad treaty between Poland, Hungary and the then Czechoslovakia, which promptly faded in importance at least until early 1994 when it was revived as a precursor to negotiations on joining the EU, principally as the Central European Free Trade Agreement. In the meantime, each country set its own tariff and non-tariff barriers against its former COMECON partners.

More than this, in certain key strategic areas, such as aviation, the new political dogma of independence prevented the emergence of strong regional groupings able to negotiate effectively on the world stage and left each country to be picked off separately by individual western airlines and plane manufacturers to the detriment of safety standards. The obvious solution to the problem of small, unprofitable east European national airlines was not the seeking of foreign investment from small, unprofitable western airlines, but the adoption of an SAS model of joint ownership and global strategic relationship. Political emotion rather than strategic reasoning ultimately, however, ruled the day.

A MIXED PICTURE OF REFORM

The picture of reform in the individual countries is mixed, with some very good stories and some very bleak ones. Given that the economic situation in central and eastern Europe was dire before the Wall came down, and that it immediately and dramatically worsened, the degree of success which Poland, Hungary and the Czech Republic have achieved in transformation and growth is remarkable and bears testimony to their determination, sacrifice and adroitness in using their own strengths and the slender resources of the West to best advantage. Nevertheless, the future of such success undoubtedly will be based on the speed with which more radical change can be effected and the speed with which the benefits can be pushed down to the person in the street.

In contrast, Russia presents a more depressing picture. Despite protestations to the contrary, by 1994 there had been no shock therapy, short or otherwise, only a relentless and inexorable decline in the standard of living and quality of life, in industrial output and other key economic indicators. The Russian reformers could point to some successes in, for example, the speed of privatisation. But, as we shall see, privatisation has been an island of reform aimed more at changing the name on the share certificate than in getting to the heart of industrial restructuring. Inflation fell in early 1994. But this was a success too late to help the reformers at the elections in 1993, although it was due almost certainly to their policies four months earlier. Unlike the successful central European countries, the Russian government became increasingly at odds with the other political institutions especially parliament. It failed to gain control over the money supply. Indeed until the amazing volte-face of the Russian Central Bank in the spring of 1994, the principal constraint on the money supply more frequently seemed to be the availability of paper on which to print the roubles, despite the genuine push for reform in government itself. Increasingly government came to represent a centrist political complexion, which itself was not represented in the way people cast their votes.

The 1993 elections were not favourable to the reformers, widely perceived to have failed, and produced one of the most preposterous neo-fascist parties to emerge in post-cold war Europe. Yet if these results were bad for individual political parties, the 1994 Russian local elections were disastrous for the continuation of democracy. Many cities or regions failed to muster the minimum turnout of the electorate required – only 25 per cent – and had to resort to extending the voting period in order to get any election result at all.

This level of apathy was not solely the result of economic failure. It was part of the continuing world disenchantment with politics and politicians but writ large, in Russia's case, by confusion and uncertainty as to whether they were in fact citizens of a single country with traditions, and what role that country played both within the CIS and further abroad. It was as if, by accepting the impoverished new world role of Russia, they had somehow lost a war and been accorded an unequal peace.

A POOR WESTERN RESPONSE

Faced with these challenges, how have world institutions and the private sector reacted to them? Our expectations and the expectations of the central and east Europeans were almost certainly excessive, based on misconceptions of the way in which world capitalism worked, the resources available, and the stodgy success which these institutions had had in keeping the peace and promoting economic development over forty-five years. These institutions were of course dominated by their shareholders and the leading politicians of the time, and were not truly independent world institutions.

In this respect, though, the 1980s seemed to be characterised by politicians who, whether you supported them or not, had a genuine view of a world political order: George Bush, Margaret Thatcher, François Mitterand and Mikhail Gorbachev all fall into this category. It is not surprising that such figures should speak in terms of a new world order, a common European homeland, or a larger European Community of nations including central and eastern Europe. Yet all fell foul of the change in mood of their domestic powerbases, as they swung away from support for the grander international vision to the concerns of domestic issues which were growing ever more pressing as recession loomed. In the 1990s, politicians emerged whose principal concerns were with domestic policy and who cut little ice as visionaries on the world stage. This discontinuity in western outlook overlapped with the fall of communism. The predisposition of the earlier politicians to see the wider picture and to take the longer view gave way to a mentality of always counting the cost and creatively trying to fulfil earlier pledges by sleight of hand. The central and east Europeans had a point in saying that the goal posts were moved halfway through the game.

Yet despite this, some institutions maintained a consistent approach. Take, for example, the IMF.

THE IMF

The IMF was founded in 1944 by agreement at Bretton Woods, New Hampshire, USA and opened for currency business in 1947.

Its mandate was a pragmatic one of bringing currency stability by preventing a return to the problems of the 1930s. At the time, there was considerable debate between the more restricted, US, pragmatic view of the IMF's role and that proposed by Keynes, which would have given it wide powers to interfere with the national economic independence of individual countries; in other words, to see it as a sort of global central bank. Its origins were, therefore, rooted in pre-war problems set within a post-war, bipolar context.

Its role in central Europe and especially in Poland, generally passed without intense criticism and may even have significantly speeded the resolve of successive Polish governments to keep to a common path of economic reform. Yet its role in Russia has been the subject of the most aggressive criticism, especially from a Harvard professor and peripatetic government adviser, Jeffrey Sachs.

Much of the debate between Sachs and the IMF echoes the original debate about the role of the IMF between its US creators and John Maynard Keynes. Sachs, for example, has damned the IMF for its narrow approach to the Russian economy, which was based on conservative lending policies, insistence on tight economic controls, a reduction of the budget deficit and limited internal interference. Sachs has argued that IMF funds could have been critical in achieving earlier stabilisation and bolstering of the reform process if more money had been spent in a more interventionist way, including support for 'non-inflationary social programmes'.

Even in the most optimistic case, however, it is doubtful whether the IMF could have provided sufficient funds either to save the Russian economy or change the political tide of voters. Indeed, in the latter case, such an avowed aim would have been anathema to much of the world community. It has, therefore, pursued a consistent policy in keeping with the circumstances of the recipients of its loans. In the case of Russia it has not been the IMF which has moved the goal posts, but the Russian government. Given the inability of the Russians to provide track record and guarantees as to fairly basic economic conditions set by the IMF, it was quite right not simply to send good money after bad. A similar criticism of EBRD's lending policy, which precipitated the crisis which brought down Jacques Attali, its first president, was similarly misplaced. Without some certainty that there were sufficient economic structures in place on the Russian side to accept and use the funds, it was right not to disburse them. Indeed, when EBRD was, in 1993-4, forced to show increased lending, it was not surprising that its bad debt provisions also showed significant increase.

Were the IMF conditions too strict and could they have been relaxed? Looked at solely from a macro-economic point of view, my response errs on the side of the IMF. To me, as a regular observer of Russian politics and economics, there was not sufficient control by the Russians over the economy to be able to deliver on prudent economic management, and not enough consistency of policy and commitment to reform where it mattered. A basic level of reform was required for any economic development and was not a reflection of particular IMF *bêtes noires*. Much of this stemmed from the inadequacies of the Russian parliamentary system and the way in which President Yeltsin failed to consolidate his position effectively after major events such as the referendum on who rules Russia. Given these circumstances, it was surely not unreasonable to expect Russia to put its house in order before being given any more funds. This, of course, they appeared able to do in April 1994 to achieve the release of US$1.5 billion from the IMF.

The anti-IMF camp has two points, however. First, it is surely correct in saying that the West's overall response was inadequate to the crisis not only in Russia but also in central and eastern Europe as a whole. The IMF was never asked, and never sought, to take the lead in co-ordinating the West's response, although by virtue of its reputation where it went others were sure to follow. Unfortunately no other organisation was asked to take this role either. As a result there was insufficient tie-in between the technical assistance projects being funded by world institutions in order to establish the infrastructure which was a pre-requisite of IMF loans, and the policies of the IMF itself.

Second, as we shall see more graphically in Chapter 7, the principal indicators used to measure the success of the countries of the region in achieving reform were the traditional macro-economic indicators, such as GDP. In a developed, stable economy where social issues are not paramount the use of such indicators to drive the economies of countries as a whole is arguably justified. In central and eastern Europe they are at best misleading, and reinforce the divergence between macro-economic success and micro-economic failure as quality of life plummets and social factors such as crime become more important.

A NEW WORLD INSTITUTION

Since the major world institutions were set up on the basis of restricted mandates, it is surely the biggest expectations' gap of all to assume that these institutions could have been able to change overnight to face an unclear and changing world situation and to adopt a new brand of economics in which GDP was a measure of social effect as well as macro-economic performance. What was needed to tackle the problem was a new world institution created from scratch or an impractical, radical overhaul of established vested interests.

The principal response to this was the European Bank for Reconstruction and Development (EBRD). Its creator, Jacques Attali, spoke as we shall later see, in an elevated fashion about how the bank was to be the new institution of the new world order. But it was neither equipped for the task or ceded the role even of *primus inter pares*. Its structure was based on existing world institutions and saw no radical departure from the politics which characterised those institutions. Its hegemony was fiercely contested by the World Bank, amongst others. This is not surprising, as it would seem that EBRD too was born out of myopia. As Baroness Thatcher's memoirs reveal, the bank was initially seen by Mitterand and Attali as a European affair and only expanded into a global institution after pressure from the G7 (Thatcher, 1994).

What was missing from all of this was an understanding that central and eastern Europe, and particularly the former USSR, was a complex web of cultures, the ability of which to respond, not only quickly but at all, to the sorts of stable institutions required to sustain economic reform was varied. Anyone could devise policies to transform a command economy into a market economy. What could not be devised and what has not been achieved quickly is to change the cultural perceptions of people to accept new political and economic institutions as if they were mature institutions. That expectations' gap is still fundamental to all our attitudes to the area.

2

Progress to Reform: the Winners and Losers

INTRODUCTION

Before examining some of the key areas of reform, such as privatisation and restructuring, it is worth trying to get an overview of what has happened to date in the region. This chapter, therefore, provides a brief snapshot as at first quarter 1994 of the progress to reform in each of the central and east European countries and tries to bring out some of the particular problems each country faces. These snapshots are based, as is customary, on the normal macro-economic criteria such as GDP. As indicated in Chapter 7, however, there are serious reservations about the appropriateness of these criteria in this context. Table 2.1 shows the ranking produced by Ernst & Young as part of its quarterly publication *Emerging Markets Profiles* and *World Link*, the journal of the World Economic Forum. The consistency with which Poland, the Czech Republic, Hungary and Slovenia come top of the rankings was matched also by figures produced by the United Nations Economic Commission for Europe.

The tables for each country have been drawn from a number of sources including PlanEcon, EIU, Reuters, OECD, EBRD, Euromoney. The GDP figure represents percentage growth over the past year. Many figures, including inflation, are still imprecise and estimated.

Table 2.1 *Individual country ratings*

	Business opportunities	Political risk	Credit rating	Status of local economy	Stability	Business infra-structure	Science & technology	Manpower	Total
Poland	1	2	2	3	2	2	3	2	17
Czech Republic	2	2	2	3	1	2	3	2	17
Hungary	3	2	2	3	2	2	3	2	19
Slovenia	4	2	2	3	2	3	4	2	22
Estonia	4	2	3	3	2	3	4	2	23
Latvia	4	2	3	3	2	4	4	2	24
Bulgaria	3	4	4	3	3	3	3	3	26
Kazakhstan	2	3	4	4	3	4	3	3	26
Russia	1	5	4	4	4	4	2	3	27
Slovakia	4	4	3	4	3	3	4	3	28
Lithuania	4	3	4	4	3	4	5	3	30
Romania	3	4	4	4	4	4	4	3	30
Belarus	3	4	4	4	4	4	4	3	30
Croatia	4	4	4	4	4	4	4	3	31
Uzbekistan	3	4	4	4	4	4	5	4	33
Kyrgystan	4	4	4	4	4	4	5	4	33
Albania	4	4	5	4	4	4	5	4	33
Ukraine	4	4	4	5	4	4	4	4	34
Azerbaijan	3	5	5	5	5	4	4	4	35
Moldova	4	4	5	5	4	5	5	4	35
Turkmenistan	4	4	5	5	4	4	5	4	35
Armenia	5	5	5	5	4	5	5	4	38
Tadzhikistan	5	5	5	5	5	5	5	4	39
Georgia	5	5	5	5	5	5	5	4	39
Former Yugoslavia	5	5	5	5	5	5	5	5	40

Key
1 = Best rating
5 = Worst rating

Business Opportunities = Size and structure of domestic market and attitude towards foreign investment
Political risk = Stability of government and market-orientated policies
Credit rating = Sovereign debt – attitude of international financial markets
Status of local economy = Domestic economic performance
Stability = Overall political and economic stability
Business infrastructure = Legal framework, professional services, telecommunications and distribution
Science & technology = Availability of, and access to, significant research resources
Manpower = Availability of significant, quality manpower

Source: *Ernst & Young/Worldlink*

POLAND

Overall Ernst & Young score	17
Population	38.5 million
GDP growth (1993)	4.0% (a)
External debt (1993)	US$34 billion (b)
Inflation (1993)	34.4% (c)
Expected GDP growth (1994)	4-5% (d)

Key
(a) EIU
(b) Reuters
(c) PlanEcon
(d) EBRD

Business opportunities

Poland consistently proves attractive in respect of business opportunities. The large size of the potential domestic market is matched by encouragement to enter, and easy access to, the opportunities available. These opportunities are generated by privatisation, by a healthy and extensive private sector and by an extremely active stock market. Good investment opportunities are being identified and there has been a significant increase in foreign investment during 1992 and 1993. Growth of actual foreign investment to 1993 is shown in Figure 2.1 below in US$ millions.

US$ millions

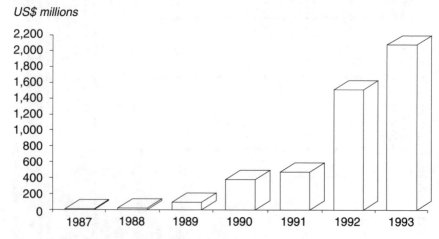

Figure 2.1 Actual foreign investment in Poland

Source: *United Nations Economic Commission for Europe*

Figures produced by EEIM for 1993, although on a different basis, suggest that by the end of 1993 the *committed* investment had reached US$10 billion. The principal sectors receiving foreign investment had been the automotive sector and general manufacturing, as well as companies operating in wholesale or retail trade.

Political risk

Despite frequent changes of government, Poland has low political risk. Although the reform process has been slowed at times by these changes, the underlying stability has remained constant even throughout the period of the short, sharp shock economic policies. To many, the nightmare scenario occurred in 1994 when a government of former communists was returned to power. Yet privatisation continued, the stock market continued to grow until April 1994, Poland concluded a very favourable debt reduction agreement with the London Club, and it made formal application to join the EU.

Credit rating

Although external debt has been high, Poland has been able to obtain significant financial support from the world's financial institutions, particularly as it has emerged from recession with a strong domestic currency. The internal convertibility of the zloty within Poland is proceeding with success and full international convertibility is likely to be achieved sooner rather than later.

As a result, in spring 1994, the new Polish government was able successfully to negotiate a 45 per cent forgiveness of debt and debt servicing from the London Club of commercial banks, with a forgiveness of a similar amount expected from the Paris Club. The outcome of these negotiations was generally regarded as generous in view of Poland's economic success. Alternatively, it should be seen as far-sighted realisation that the Polish economy could still have been pushed back into recession by excessive debt burdens.

Status of local economy

Unemployment at some 16 per cent remains high, as does inflation.

Nevertheless, there are strong signs of optimism in the way in which economic reforms have been successful particularly in encouraging the growth of the private sector. Growth in 1994 is expected to be 4-5 per cent of GDP.

Stability

Public disenchantment with the reform process is a problem and can be seen in the election of former communists to government. This is largely due to the effects being felt throughout the economy as Poland comes out of recession.

Business infrastructure

Poland's progress can be seen clearly in the significant improvements in business infrastructure. The legal and regulatory framework is substantially developed. Professional services are available and the internal distribution system is improving. The banking system continues to be reformed. Telecommunications are still difficult outside Warsaw.

Science & technology and manpower

Poland has potential research and development capabilities which could be developed further. It has a surplus of skilled workers in many areas. Although Poland has a history of trade union unrest, this has generally not spilled over into the private sector.

Poland is widely expected to retain a lower wage cost base for longer than its central European neighbours.

CZECH REPUBLIC

Overall Ernst & Young score	17
Population	10.3 million
GDP growth (1993)	0% (e)
External debt (1993)	US$9 billion (e)
Inflation (1993)	21.9% (e)
Expected GDP growth (1994)	1-6% (e), (f)

Key
(e) OECD
(f) UNESCO

Business opportunities

Clearly the size of the potential domestic market in the Czech Republic is much smaller than that in Poland. Nevertheless, the Czech Republic has been successful in attracting foreign investment. Such investment has been attracted without the provision of fiscal or other incentives and despite growing wage rates and relatively high, real estate costs. This testifies to the perceived strength of the local economy.

The principal sector of investment has been the automotive sector. However, investment has also been widely spread across a number of other sectors from brewing to engineering. Of all the central and east European countries, recent statistics (EEIM) suggest that the Czech Republic has the largest, committed amount of foreign investment.

Growth of Foreign Direct Investment in the Czech Republic

US$ millions

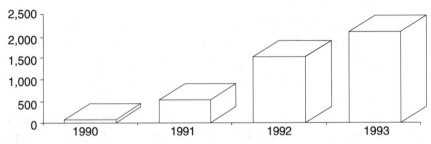

Figure 2.2 Foreign investment in the Czech Republic

Source: *United Nations Economic Commission for Europe*

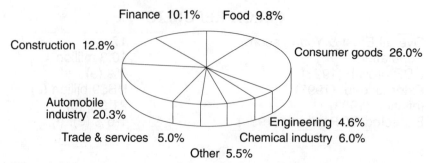

Figure 2.2a Breakdown of foreign investment in the Czech Republic by industry sector

Source: *United Nations Economic Commission for Europe*

Political risk

The Czech Republic is widely regarded as the most politically stable of the Visegrad countries. Its charismatic Prime Minister, Vaclav Klaus, has pursued a consistent set of reform policies best described as 'managed Thatcherism'. This level of focus and imagination in reform measures, such as voucher privatisation, has kept the momentum of reform alive.

Credit ranking

The Czech Republic has high foreign currency reserves and a successful internal convertibility, which is likely to lead to full convertibility in the short term. A pragmatic and cautious attitude to foreign aid and assistance has kept the Czech Republic's external debt low.

Status of local economy

Inflation is expected to fall in 1994 to no more than 10 per cent. On the other hand, unemployment will be likely to increase from its current level of 3 per cent. Many commentators have feared an increase in unemployment to Polish levels as post-privatisation restructuring occurs. However, recent estimates are more optimistic that the unemployment over-hang has been contained at about 6 per cent by the development of service industries. Overall growth is expected for 1994.

Stability

The public appears to have accepted the reforms and the Czech Republic presents an economically stable face. Much of this is likely to be due to the way in which public enthusiasm was channelled at an early stage into the successful voucher privatisation programme, providing most Czechs with a real feeling of participation.

Business infrastructure

Business infrastructure is now extremely well developed, with significant plans for new high-speed rail and road networks across the country. Telecommunications are good and the level of business sophistication is high.

Science & technology and manpower

As with Poland and Hungary, there are significant research and development opportunities and skilled workers are generally westernised in work attitudes. However, given the low level of unemployment, the availability of workers can be patchy. In addition, wage costs are being bid up, quickly reducing some of the country's overall competitive advantage.

HUNGARY

Overall Ernst & Young score	17
Population	10.29 million
GDP growth (1993)	-1.0%
External debt (1993)	US$24 billion (g)
Inflation (1993)	20-5% (b), (c)
Expected GDP growth (1994)	1% (a)

Key
(a) EIU
(b) Reuters
(c) PlanEcon
(g) Euromoney

Business opportunities

Hungary has clearly benefited significantly from its positive, reformist image in the West and the efforts it has made to attract foreign investment. There is a growing suspicion, however, that given the size of the country, the best business opportunities may already have gone and what is left is often unattractive given the reluctance of the government to restructure and the half-hearted approach to privatisation.

Recent figures of committed funds from foreign investors (EEIM) suggest that Hungary has now fallen behind both Poland and the Czech Republic. In addition, while multi-million dollar investment has been forthcoming, for example General Electric's investment in Tungsram, the average size of investments has fallen over recent years. The principal sectors for foreign investment have been automotive, electronics, food production and property.

Political risk

Hungary remains a politically stable country despite increasing apathy from the population and the activities of a small minority of local extremists. The elections in 1994 returned a government of former communists but, as with Poland, no significant changes are likely to result. A point of political uncertainty remains the attitude towards ethnic Hungarians living in Romania, Slovakia and the former Yugoslavia.

Credit rating

Despite the highest per capita debt in the region, Hungarian credit remains good and government bond issues are generally well accepted by the market. This is partly based on the building-up of foreign currency earnings, but also on the respect which the National Bank of Hungary has earned in international financial markets.

Status of local economy

The local economy suffers significantly in pre-election periods. In 1994, however, it has suffered more from the ambivalent attitude of the Hungarian government to deep economic reform. This may sound surprising in view of Hungary's reputation; but beneath the surface there has been a reluctance to restructure and continuing battles with foreign advisers, which show underlying uncertainty in a full commitment to reform. Nevertheless, despite relatively high inflation, some growth is predicted for 1994.

Stability

Overall, Hungary remains a stable country. However, continuing government indecision and a worsening of the standard of living could see a rise in extremist parties, fuelled also by concern over the plight of ethnic Hungarians in neighbouring countries.

Business infrastructure

There has been considerable development of the business infrastructure. This has included a well-developed legal and regulatory framework, as well as an overall successful re-orientation of attitudes and trade towards the West. Basic infrastructure, such as telecommunications and transport networks, has also been improved.

Science & technology and manpower

As with Poland and the Czech Republic, Hungary has potential for research and development and availability of skilled labour, with increasingly western attitudes to work ethics.

SLOVENIA

Overall Ernst & Young score	22
Population	2 million
GDP growth (1993)	-1.0% (a)
External debt (1993)	U$1.9 billion (d)
Inflation (1993)	34.0% (a)
Expected GDP growth (1994)	1.0% (a)

Key
(a) EIU
(d) EBRD

Business opportunities

Slovenia is the forgotten jewel in the former Yugoslavia which has encouraged considerable foreign investment, especially from Austria, despite a small domestic market. A strong commitment to reform has been evidenced.

Political risk

A very high level of political stability is evident, with agreement cross-party on the essentials of economic reform.

Credit rating

Good levels of foreign currency reserves are supporting international assistance to the committed reform process.

Status of local economy

Significant signs of improvement include reorientation of exports towards the EU, tight monetary policy and a reduction in inflation, together with limited industrial recovery.

Business infrastructure

Business infrastructure is good and increasingly well-integrated into the West.

Science & technology and manpower

Limited research and development capability are available; but skilled labour and solid work ethics are present.

ESTONIA

Overall Ernst & Young score	23
Population	1.56 million
GDP growth (1993)	-2.3% (a)
External debt (1993)	US$198 million (d)
Inflation (1993)	38.4% (a)
Expected GDP growth (1994)	3% (a)

Key
(a) EIU
(d) EBRD

Business opportunities

The internal market of Estonia is of necessity small. However, close links with the Nordic countries have provided significant levels of investment.

Political risk

Political risk is probably now at its lowest since independence. Confidence in its international position has produced relaxation in rules governing citizenship and an overall reduction in tension. Disillusionment with the reform process is also easing.

Credit rating

With international support, Estonia has successfully introduced its own currency which is convertible within the region. Foreign currency reserves are increasing.

Status of local economy

Despite privatisation moving ahead, restructuring of industry is still needed and a lack of management skills is acutely felt. Nevertheless, the private sector now accounts for 33 per cent of industrial production, and growth is forecast for 1994.

Stability

Low living standards may give cause for concern. However, Estonia is now substantially stable.

Business infrastructure

Investment is still required in transportation and tele-communications; but, business infrastructure has now significantly improved.

Science & technology and manpower

There is limited scope for research and development but skilled manpower is available.

LATVIA

Overall Ernst & Young score	24
Population	2.58 million
GDP growth (1993)	-10.0% (a)
External debt (1993)	N/A
Inflation (1993)	111.0% (a)
Expected GDP growth (1994)	-5.0% (a)

Key
(a) EIU

Business opportunities

While the Latvian domestic market is small, it is increasingly being integrated into a Nordic sphere of influence which is providing investment.

Political risk

There are few areas of political risk. The issue of ethnic Russians located in Latvia is gradually being resolved.

Credit rating

International support and a tight monetary policy have allowed the introduction successfully of its own currency. Inflation has been falling and foreign currency reserves increasing.

Status of local economy

Industrial output is declining in an environment where privatisation is at its early stages. Popular disenchantment with the reforms appears to be passing. However, it has been difficult to reorientate trade away from the former USSR and into western markets.

Stability

Overall, stability is being maintained by a visible improvement in life-styles and economic activity, which is encouraging entrepreneurial activity.

Business infrastructure

Good communications with Europe disguise the need for more investment in underlying infrastructure.

Science & technology and manpower

Few research and development opportunities are likely, but skilled manpower is likely to be available except for management positions.

BULGARIA

Overall Ernst & Young score	26
Population	8.42 million
GDP growth (1993)	-4.0% (a)
External debt (1993)	US$11.7 million (d)
Inflation (1993)	64% (c)
Expected GDP growth (1994)	0% (a)

Key
(a) EIU
(c) PlanEcon
(d) EBRD

Business opportunities

Although the domestic market is relatively small, it is clear that Bulgaria has not maximised its foreign investment opportunities. Outside the CIS, Bulgaria and Romania have significantly fallen behind the other central European countries. Many multinationals have toe-holds in Bulgaria but the indecisive attitude of the government to reform, and especially privatisation, has prevented further investment even in natural resources, high technology products and tourism in which Bulgaria could expand.

Political risk

Bulgaria has low political risk despite internal divisions over the direction and pace of reform. It is currently suffering, however, as a result of the war in the former Yugoslavia.

Credit ranking

Despite a weak economy and a negative trade balance, Bulgaria has continuing involvement with the IMF and World Bank and has negotiated significant debt forgiveness with the London Club.

Status of local economy

The economy has been affected by the war in the former Yugoslavia. However, a private sector is now beginning to flourish despite unemployment, inflation and a lack of restructuring in the State sector.

Stability

Active aid and technical assistance have faltered pending resolution by the Bulgarian government of its reform programme. Given the underlying weakness of the economy, economic stability may need to be watched carefully.

Business infrastructure

Legislative reform has been active in many key areas. Basic business infrastructure has significantly improved, although concerns over energy supply are still present.

Science & technology and manpower

There are good possibilities for research and development and a ready supply of inexpensive, skilled workers.

KAZAKHSTAN

Overall Ernst & Young score	26
Population	17.1 million
GDP growth (1993)	-12.9% (a)
External debt (1993)	(h)
Inflation (1993)	2,265% (a)
Expected GDP growth (1994)	-10.0% (a)

Key

(a) EIU

(h) Figures for the external debt position of former USSR Republics are confused by the amounts owing in respect of former Soviet debt.

Business opportunities

Kazakhstan has been the principal beneficiary of foreign investment in the CIS outside Russia. Recent statistics suggest that the level of committed, cumulative investment as at 31 December 1993 was not far short of that in Russia. Most of this, as with Russia, has been committed to the oil and gas sector, but with significant investments also in minerals and tobacco. Oil and gas opportunities are, however, bedevilled by issues of pipe-line transportation.

The potential for business opportunities is therefore great, but the land-locked location does create difficulty for market access.

Political risk

Political risk is currently low after parliamentary elections (criticised in the West) returned a pro-Presidential government. President Nazarbaev has retained an effective grip on power and adroitly managed external, as well as internal, political issues including the large ethnic Russian population.

Credit rating

There is considerable international support for Kazakhstan. However, to a large extent this is based on the wealth potential of its energy resources. Realising these resources is, therefore, likely to be essential.

Status of local economy

Although inflation is still high and industrial production falling, there is overall optimism that economic reform will succeed. Privatisation is now moving ahead both in respect of a mass privatisation programme and also case-by-case privatisations of individual enterprises.

Stability

The widely-held regard for Kazakhstan's stability is based principally on the character and reputation of President Nazarbaev. However, the issue of who will eventually succeed him and whether that stability can be maintained is open to question and depends on how quickly established political institutions are allowed to mature into a more dominant role.

Business infrastructure

Business infrastructure overall is steadily improving especially in Almaty.

Science & technology and manpower

Good research and development opportunities exist. Skilled workers are available but cultural differences should not be ignored.

RUSSIA

Overall Ernst & Young score	27
Population	148.77 million
GDP growth (1993)	-12.0% (a)
External debt (1993)	US$80 billion (b)
Inflation (1993)	700-1,000% (c), (a)
Expected GDP growth (1994)	-9.0% (a)

Key
(a) EIU
(b) Reuters
(c) PlanEcon

Business opportunities

The enigma of Russia can be seen in its enormous potential for business opportunities and the difficulty of realising the potential. The size of the potential domestic markets and the strengths in natural resources have, not surprisingly, made Russia a target for much multinational interest.

While Russia has in the past received significant foreign investment, the difficulties of doing business there in a confused political environment and the ambivalent attitude to reform is resulting in more investment going into the other CIS Republics as a whole than into Russia (as shown by EEIM).

Within Russia the principal investment sectors have been oil and gas, transportation (including automotive and aviation), leisure and hotels and property. Indeed, committed figures of cumulative foreign investment as at 31 December 1993 showed that investment in the oil and gas sectors accounted for over 50 per cent of total investment made by just 12 per cent of companies investing there. Many of these are, according to anecdotal evidence, now increasingly looking to Kazakhstan and Azerbaijan for earlier investment opportunities: 40 per cent of total investment has come from one country, the USA.

Political risk

Russia cannot be described as a politically stable country. Internal strife between nationalists/communists and reformers has not been settled and is likely to continue. The reformers are generally discredited in the country and are unlikely to be able to secure a parliamentary majority in the short-medium term. The government's brand of centrist politics is not reflected in the composition of parliament and is, therefore, likely to lead to continued political conflict. President Yeltsin increasingly creates the impression of a lame-duck President. In the country, widespread political apathy is based on continuing economic disintegration.

Credit rating

Not surprisingly, international institutions have been cautious in making funds available for a country in such political disarray. However, in early 1994 the Central Bank, which until then had pursued a conservative policy of high subsidies and the printing of money, fell in line with a tight monetary policy in order to secure external support, particularly from the IMF.

Status of local economy

Despite the discredited perception of the reformers, reform policies have had some effect. There is generally a four-month lag in Russia between policy change and effect. The fall in inflation in early 1994 was, therefore, likely to be the first signs of economic success in the reform process.

However, subsequently industrial production has collapsed and widespread unemployment only averted by a continuation of central subsidies. This, together with the growth of serious crime and corruption has undermined the ability of reforms to take root, although the commitment of the government to reform is now not generally doubted.

Stability

Stability internally remains fragile. Increasing apathy, a loss of direction and an erosion of Russian traditions and culture have produced a level of dissatisfaction which would not take much to ignite, either from concern for ethnic Russians elsewhere in the CIS or from concern for the worsening economy.

Nevertheless, Russia has an astonishing ability to surprise, and stability may be bought at the cost of long-term flexibility to manoeuvre out of the current economic situation.

Business infrastructure

Business infrastructure is by no means disastrous. Despite poor official infrastructure there has been a rapid development, for example, of telecommunications activity in the private sector. Nevertheless, significant bureaucracy does impede most operations. Crime and the 'Mafia' are perceived problems.

Science & technology and manpower

Significant research and development opportunities exist in the many first-class research institutes. Skilled workers can usually easily be found but many business skills and western work ethics are not present.

SLOVAKIA

Overall Ernst & Young score	28
Population	5.3 million
GDP growth (1993)	0.5% (a)
External debt (1993)	US$3.227 billion (b)
Inflation (1993)	25.3% (c)
Expected GDP growth (1994)	2.0% (a)

Key
(a) EIU
(b) Reuters
(c) PlanEcon

Business opportunities

Business opportunities in Slovakia should not be ignored despite the small size of the market and the balance of industry towards heavy industry and defence.

Political risk

Following the split with the Czech Republic, internal Slovak politics have been fluid, resulting in the defeat of the Meciar government in spring 1994. Dispute with Hungary continued over Hungarian minorities and development on the Danube. Relations with the Czech Republic have also been strained.

Credit rating

A low external debt position probably accurately reflects abilities to service loans. However, internal convertibility is still working. Further devaluations of the Slovak crown are expected.

Status of local economy

As predicted, Slovakia has not done particularly well following the split with the Czech Republic. There is high unemployment and inflation, and production continues to fall. Trade with the Czech Republic has also fallen.

Stability

A lack of clear and consistent government policy has not helped stabilise the economy and there is no clear economic strategy.

Business infrastructure

Business infrastructure is relatively good including professional services and telecommunications.

Science & technology and manpower

Some good opportunities for research and development exist. An accessible, skilled workforce is available.

BELARUS

Overall Ernst & Young score	30
Population	10.3 million
GDP growth (1993)	10% (a)
External debt (1993)	US$524.7 million (a)
Inflation (1993)	1,500% (a)
Expected GDP growth (1994)	1.7% (c)

Key
(a) EIU
(c) PlanEcon

Business opportunities

Belarus has a strong industrial base of potential interest to foreign investors. However, in reality few investors have located in the country concerned by the levels of pollution, especially from Chernobyl, and the uncertain state of an economy reliant on the import of raw materials from other CIS states. At 1 July 1993 Poland was the largest foreign investor measured by numbers of foreign investments made.

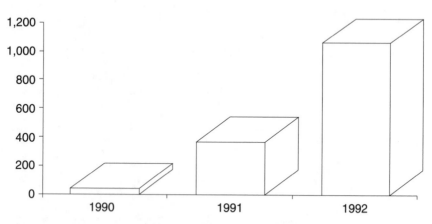

Figure 2.3 Actual numbers of foreign investments in Belarus

Source: *United Nations Economic Commission for Europe*

The principal areas of industrial activity in Belarus are artificial fibres, agricultural tractors, mineral fertilisers, plastics, metal equipment and agricultural produce.

Political risk

The government is hesitant about carrying out economic reforms although it has recently embarked on a mass privatisation programme. There has been tension between nationalists opposed to monetary union with Russia and the largely conservative government which seemed only reluctantly to accept independence on the break-up of the USSR.

Credit rating

International credit rating has not been high as international financial institutions have been concerned over the slow pace of reform. In addition, the currency union negotiated with Russia is unlikely to benefit either country and effectively ensures that Belarus will be regarded with the same eyes as Russia.

Status of local economy

The currency union with Russia is also likely to restrict the country's ability to control many aspects of its own economy; yet, in return, it is expected to provide access to reliable and cheap energy imports.

However, overall inflation remains high in an economic environment little changed from the Soviet period and with continuing subsidies of State enterprises.

Stability

Although the population has a mixed attitude to market reform, support for an equally mixed-attitude government is being undermined by falling living standards and nationalist tensions.

Business infrastructure

Business infrastructure is being developed slowly. A substantial body of legislation has been drafted but, even where enacted, is only partially implemented.

Science & technology and manpower

Belarus's research and development capabilities are generally limited. It has a ready supply of skilled workers for joint venture projects.

LITHUANIA

Overall Ernst & Young score	30
Population	3.76 million
GDP growth (1993)	-9.4% (a)
External debt (1993)	US$400 million (i)
Inflation (1993)	400% (a)
Expected GDP growth (1994)	4.3% (c)

Key
(a) EIU
(c) PlanEcon
(i) Novecon News Agency

Business opportunities

Despite a small domestic market, Lithuania has potentially interesting niche opportunities which are likely to fall within the ambit of the Nordic countries.

Political risk

Notwithstanding a more gradual approach to reform, disillusionment with the reform process is easing.

Credit rating

A new, national currency was successfully introduced and has remained stable with support from international financial institutions.

Status of local economy

Industry needs restructuring but there is a severe shortage of management skills. Industrial output continues to fall and unemployment to rise, which will in part be offset by an expanding private sector.

Business infrastructure

Business infrastructure generally requires considerable investment, including transportation and telecommunications.

Science & technology and manpower

Limited access to research and development and to skilled workers are available.

ROMANIA

Overall Ernst & Young score	30
Population	23 million
GDP growth (1993)	0% (a)
External debt (1993)	US$3.3 billion (k)
Inflation (1993)	300% (c)
Expected GDP growth (1994)	1.0% (a)

Key
(a) EIU
(c) PlanEcon
(k) Economic Bulletin for Europe, UN

Business opportunities

Considerable potential business opportunities are frequently frustrated by the slow and faltering pace of reform and shortages of energy and other raw materials. Nevertheless, Romania has significant industrial, agricultural and possibly even energy opportunities. Most of these have been the subject of small-scale capital investments from overseas which have been restricted to a large number of small investments of often an average size of no more than US$25,000.

Political risk

The possibility of political risk increasing must be considered following earlier waves of strikes and the militancy of some unions. The government is still substantially composed of former communists who have been active in slowing the pace of reform.

Credit rating

Starting from an historically low debt position, Romania has been borrowing internationally and is supported by the IMF against relatively low foreign currency reserves.

Status of local economy

The transition to a market economy is proving painfully slow and the economy is still in recession. Unemployment and inflation both remain high. Privatisation provides a clear example of the problem with progress being slowed by former communists with continuing vested interests.

Stability

The threat of social and political unrest remains a real possibility as the negative side of the economy continues to hold sway. The slow pace of reform must also eventually delay further international support.

Business infrastructure

A relatively comprehensive legal framework is in place. However, current infrastructure as a whole is still extremely poor and will require western involvement.

Science & technology and manpower

There are limited opportunities for research and development and for obtaining skilled workers.

CROATIA

Overall Ernst & Young score	31
Population	4.784 million
GDP growth (1993)	-11% (a)
External debt (1993)	US$2.5 billion (k)
Inflation (1993)	1,517% (a)
Expected GDP growth (1994)	N/A

Key
(a) EIU
(k) Economic Bulletin for Europe, UN

Business opportunities

There are potentially good opportunities in Croatia but these are unlikely to be realised until the war in the former Yugoslavia has ceased and the government takes a less ambiguous attitude to foreign investment.

Political risk

The clear political risk lies in the instability of the former Yugoslavia as a whole, and in the ability of the government to deliver reform.

Credit rating

Agreement with the IMF is being sought to begin the process of reform and reconstruction.

Status of local economy

A stabilisation programme and strict monetary policy have sharply reduced inflation and may produce growth in 1994.

Business infrastructure

Prior to the civil war Croatia generally had good infrastructure. A period of reconstruction will inevitably be required.

Science & technology and manpower

There are few opportunities for research and development. Skilled labour is likely to be plentiful in due course.

UZBEKISTAN

Overall Ernst & Young score	31
Population	21.5 million
GDP growth (1993)	-10.0% (a)
External debt (1993)	(h)
Inflation (1993)	700% (d)
Expected GDP growth (1994)	2.2% (c)

Key
(a) EIU
(c) PlanEcon
(d) EBRD
(h) Figures for the external debt position of former USSR Republics are confused by the amounts owing in respect of former Soviet debt.

Business opportunities

Uzbekistan has attracted substantial foreign investment and now ranks behind only Russia and Kazakhstan in terms of committed funds. Opportunities exist across a wide range of industries including agriculture, textiles, raw materials and mining. These opportunities are increasingly available under new market reforms introduced.

Political risk

The government of Uzbekistan is a reformed communist one but with a chequered history in relation to human rights allegations and reforms. There is potential for increased political risk if these factors are not addressed.

Credit rating

Substantial reserves of gas and gold could support a higher credit rating if economic reform progresses.

Status of local economy

Some improvements have been seen in industrial production recently. However, the cotton mono-culture has made Uzbekistan dependent on food imports.

Stability

Muslim fundamentalism and the spillover of conflicts in neighbouring States are the most likely cause of future instability.

Business infrastructure

Considerable infrastructure improvement is required. However, the regulatory environment is being closely controlled.

Science & technology and manpower

There are limited opportunities for research and development and for acquiring skilled workers.

ALBANIA

Overall Ernst & Young score	33
Population	3.49 million
GDP growth (1993)	6.0% (a)
External debt (1993)	US$624 million (b)
Inflation (1993)	30.9% (b)
Expected GDP growth (1994)	4.0% (a)

Key
(a) EIU
(b) Reuters

Business opportunities

Considering its small size, Albania is making the most of its natural mineral resources and tourist areas to develop investment. This is being encouraged by the government but few substantial investments have yet been made.

Political risk

Political risk is at an all-time low. The government continues to enjoy wide popular support. The economic crisis appears to have been stabilised and law and order is being maintained.

Credit rating

International debt is minimal as is the country's ability to repay more significant amounts. Nevertheless, the IMF is providing credits.

Status of local economy

Economic recovery has begun. Although industry is still collapsed, agricultural output is increasing after the successful privatisation of land.

Stability

Despite low living standards and the need for additional food aid, the country remains stable.

Business infrastructure

A very poor business infrastructure is deterring foreign investment. Significant investment in the infrastructure is required after decades of international isolation.

Science & technology and manpower

Little opportunity for research and development exists and skilled manpower is limited.

KYRGYSTAN

Overall Ernst & Young score	33
Population	4.5 million
GDP growth (1993)	-13.0% (a)
External debt (1993)	US$334.4 million (c)
Inflation (1993)	1,300% (a)
Expected GDP growth (1994)	3.3% (c)

Key
(a) EIU
(c) PlanEcon

Business opportunities

Despite favourable foreign investment legislation and active government encouragement, Kyrgystan has probably not received its fair share of foreign investment despite the small size of its industrial base and the large extent of its agricultural sector. Its dependence on central Soviet export mechanisms has significantly eroded exports in the post-USSR period. Much of the industrial base was related to the defence sector which has further exacerbated the problem.

In the agricultural sector, textiles, tobacco and dairy products have dominated, but even these require capital investment. Kyrgystan was, for example, the USSR's principal tobacco producer.

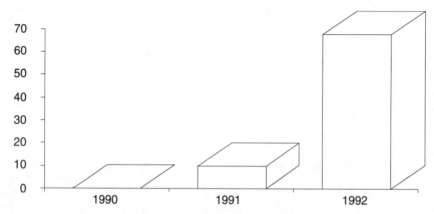

Figure 2.4 Actual numbers of foreign investors in Kyrgystan

Source: *United Nations Economic Commission for Europe*

Political risk

Although there has been tension between presidential authority and parliamentary authority, the overall level of political risk has not been significant. The country has received substantial praise internationally and has been focused in its reforms. Nevertheless, decreasing standards of living may prove difficult for the population to bear over time.

Credit rating

Kyrgystan has low foreign currency reserves. However, its commitment to reform and the focused way it has approached it, ensured that it was the first CIS State to be admitted to the IMF and the World Bank. Kyrgystan was also the first CIS State to leave the rouble zone with financial credits from the IMF.

Status of local economy

Output continues to decline. However, the second wave of reform already started has concentrated on micro-economic reform which appears to be slowing the decline.

Stability

The continued involvement of international funds has no doubt reinforced stability. Serious tensions could arise if decline continues.

Business infrastructure

As the most reform-minded of the CIS states, legislation has been introduced to encourage foreign investment and privatisation. Hydro-electric projects are now high on the list of priorities in order to ensure a domestic source of energy.

Science & technology and manpower

There are probably insignificant research and development opportunities given the small size of the industrial base. Skilled workers, and especially western-orientated managers, will be difficult to find given the reliance on former Soviet institutions to conduct all overseas trading activities.

UKRAINE

Overall Ernst & Young score	33
Population	52.1 million
GDP growth (1993)	-13.2% (a)
External debt (1993)	(h)
Inflation (1993)	3,200% (a)
Expected GDP growth (1994)	-10.0% (a)

Key

(a) EIU

(h) Figures for the external debt position of former USSR Republics are confused by the amounts owing in respect of former Soviet debt.

Business opportunities

Although well-endowed with natural resources, including coal and agricultural land, foreign investment in Ukraine has been constrained by political uncertainty and it has now, according to recent statistics, slipped behind Uzbekistan in terms of committed investment funds. Concerns have also been raised in respect of pollution levels. Nevertheless, it does have a large market for consumer goods.

Political risk

Political risk is high both internally between reformers and conservatives, Ukrainians and Russians, and externally in its relations with Russia. The Crimea is ready to become fully independent of Ukraine. Relations with Russia over payment for energy have resulted in gas being denied export from Russia to Ukraine.

Credit rating

Hyperinflation and a decline in energy resources have crippled Ukraine's potential world financial standing and will require more than IMF credits to sustain a faltering reform programme.

Status of local economy

Production has fallen in almost all sectors and there are widespread shortages of raw materials and other imports.

Stability

Currently Ukraine must be regarded as highly unstable. Internal divisions and poverty are exacerbated by external disagreements with Russia.

Business infrastructure

Good transport links to the West conceal a business infrastructure substantially inadequate to cope with the pressures made on it.

Science & technology and manpower

Good research and development opportunities are present. Skilled manpower is available from a large, well-educated workforce.

AZERBAIJAN

Overall Ernst & Young score	34
Population	7.20 million
GDP growth (1993)	-10.0% (a)
External debt (1993)	(h)
Inflation (1993)	2,000% (a)
Expected GDP growth (1994)	4.7% (c)

KEY
(a) EIU
(c) PlanEcon
(h) Figures for the external debt position of former USSR Republics are confused by the amounts owing in respect of former Soviet debt.

Business opportunities

The principal business opportunities lie within the oil and gas and agricultural sectors. However, government attention has not significantly been focused on the economy in view of the conflict with Armenia. Strong trading links have been built up with Iran and Turkey. Overall attitudes to, and expectations of, negotiations with foreign parties appear unrealistic.

Political risk

Although significantly more stable under President Aliyev, the continuing conflict with Armenia and the large number of refugees from the conflict are cause for concern.

Credit rating

Credit rating in the medium-long term could be good if oil revenues are realised quickly and effectively.

Status of local economy

The local economy has contracted because of the conflict and there are shortages of energy and raw materials.

Stability

Critical to stability will be an early end to the conflict and a concentration on economic reform, including resettlement of war refugees.

Business infrastructure

Although laws are often in place, successive governments have made negotiations difficult. Infrastructure, even for the oil and gas sector, needs developing.

Science & technology and manpower

Few opportunities for research and development and limited availability of skilled labour.

TURKMENISTAN, ARMENIA, TADZHIKISTAN, GEORGIA AND MOLDOVA

Turkmenistan

Overall Ernst & Young score	35
Population	3.89 million
GDP growth (1993)	-5.0% (d)
External debt (1993)	(h)
Inflation (1993)	1,500% (a)
Expected GDP growth (1994)	4.5% (c)

Key
(a) EIU
(c) PlanEcon
(d) EBRD
(h) Figures for the external debt position of former USSR Republics are confused by the amounts owing in respect of former Soviet debt.

Armenia

Overall Ernst & Young score	38
Population	3.7 million
GDP growth (1993)	-10.0%
External debt (1993)	(h)
Inflation (1993)	85.2%
Expected GDP growth (1994)	8.2% (c)

Key
(c) PlanEcon
(h) Figures for the external debt position of former USSR Republics are confused by the amounts owing in respect of former Soviet debt.

Tadzhikistan

Overall Ernst & Young score	39
Population	5.6 million
GDP growth (1993)	-10.0%
External debt (1993)	
Inflation (1993)	2,000%
Expected GDP growth (1994)	2.7% (c)

Key
(c) PlanEcon

Georgia

Overall Ernst & Young score	39
Population	5.4 million
GDP growth (1993)	-10.0%
External debt (1993)	
Inflation (1993)	2,000%
Expected GDP growth (1994)	5.3% (c)

Key
(c) PlanEcon

Moldova

Overall Ernst & Young score	35
Population	4.4 million
GDP growth (1993)	-10.0%
External debt (1993)	US$500 million
Inflation (1993)	3,200% (a)
Expected GDP growth (1994)	3.8% (c)

Key
(a) EIU
(c) PlanEcon

Business opportunities

All five countries present limited business opportunities, particularly in view of the conflicts in Armenia, Georgia and Tadzhikistan. In all but Tadzhikistan, foreign investment has been encouraged but has not materialised in significant quantities. Turkmenistan has certain advantages in its natural energy resources.

Political risk

Moldova and Turkmenistan provide better political risk than the other three where there is armed conflict either internally or with neighbouring countries. Moldova too has internal problems in relation to the self-proclaimed Dnestr region, while Turkmenistan's political stability appears to rest on a Soviet-style personality cult surrounding the President.

Credit rating

None of the countries, except Turkmenistan, has significant, international credit rating in current circumstances.

Status of local economy

All countries, again with the exception of Turkmenistan, have poorly developed local economies and only limited focus on effective reform.

Stability

Turkmenistan is the exception in terms of overall stability. The other countries clearly have continuing declines in standards of living.

Business infrastructure

Infrastructure in Moldova and Turkmenistan is improving with relatively good telecommunications and banking networks for the area. In the other countries, business infrastructure remains disrupted.

Science & technology and manpower

There is little scope for research and development and overall patchy access to skilled labour.

3

The Transfer of Know How

While the progress of reform outlined in Chapter 2 has considerably been aided by the provision of loans from financial institutions and commercial banks, the transfer of the know how to make the loans work effectively has been made through technical assistance. Technical assistance includes, typically, studies on the development of infrastructure, especially financial infrastructure, and the implementation of reform.

By the beginning of 1994, total commitments for technical assistance for the development of central and eastern Europe, including the CIS, amounted to some US$10 billion. Much of this had been made available under arrangements put into place by the G7 or through the principal development agencies involved in central and eastern Europe – EBRD, EU, and the World Bank. Individual governments had also pledged sums on a bilateral basis, the best known of which are US AID and the British Know How Fund.

Just what did we expect to happen in the region as a result of this funding? Has the progress outlined in Chapter 2 represented value for money and has it been effective? Table 3.1 below sets out the details of the major funding sources.

To answer these questions, of course, it is necessary to have a clear idea of the objectives each institution had in making the funds available. All would probably agree that the general objective of the funds is to assist in the transformation of the economies of central and eastern Europe into market economies. As Chapter 2 has shown, this has partially been achieved. But beyond this, there is little in the way of agreement, for example, of the extent to which technical assistance should support political and social reform, or how closely it should be allied to the overall reform programmes instituted by the IMF and the creditor nations and institutions.

Some institutions clearly believed that they had an almost divine role. Take the EBRD under its former management, for example.

In his inaugural speech to the EBRD's Board of Governors, Jacques Attali, its first president, claimed that the EBRD was the 'first institution' of the post cold-war period: the first institution of a united Europe; and, the first institution of the new world order (Attali, 1991). He hoped it would bring into existence what some were calling the 'common home', and, in any event, he thought it would provide a natural framework for learning continental solidarity and would be the natural forum for the great debates that would lead to the formation of a continental economic space: and these, were the exaggerated claims for what was nothing more than a bank.

Table 3.1 *Principal providers of technical assistance*

	Amount available 1993	*Principal emphasis*
EU Phare	ECU 1.040 billion	Economic restructuring and democratic reform
EU Tacis	ECU 0.6 billion	Acceleration of economic reform process
World Bank	US$306 million	Energy, agriculture, transportation, industry, finance, education
EBRD	ECU 84.9 million (a)	Energy, privatisation, finance, transport, environment, telecomms, SMEs restructuring, legal, social, tourism, industry
UK KHF	£48.3 million	Banking & finance, management & training, small businesses, local government, health, agriculture
US AID	US$492.8 million	Privatisation, agriculture, public administration, training

Key
(a) EBRD has no technical assistance funds of its own: funds are provided by multilateral and bilateral donors under special arrangements.

At a more international level the story is the same. Each US President after each G7 has spoken about the momentous changes occurring in the region and in the irreversibility of the process that the West is now helping, particularly the CIS, to undertake. Yet the aftermath of these expressions of solidarity and support have been the August 1991 coup against Mikhail Gorbachov, an indecisive referendum for President Yeltsin, the shelling of the Russian White House and the rise of extreme fascists. Solidarity and moral support appear not to have been particularly effective.

Unusually, only the EU's PHARE and TACIS programmes appear to have been more restrained in their pledges, at least according to their own literature (PHARE, 1992). Even they, however, could not resist one boast in saying that 'the PHARE programme has become synonymous with western assistance as a whole', a boast which many other technical assistance programmes must now regard as almost libellous!

The language used by politicians and world leaders whenever new amounts of money were made available significantly raised expectations on the central and east European side that there was going to be an immediate effect and an immediate improvement in their economies and ways of life. The individual programmes were, however, set up to achieve much more modest and circumspect aims. After the rhetoric which implied sweeping changes to these economies, it was something of a shock for them to find money being poured into accountancy. Therefore there was, in my opinion, a major expectations' gap between what the programmes could deliver and what the recipients of the assistance in central and eastern Europe itself had come to expect. That expectations' gap has been extremely poorly managed by politicians from both the East and the West. One only has to look at the catalogue of events in Russia already described to see a very vivid continuing example of this.

POLITICS HAS NOT KEPT PACE

If most technical assistance has been directed towards economic reform, has this left political institutions to follow at a much slower pace? Is there a divergence between economic advancement and political stability and even the understanding of voters as to which economic reforms go with which political parties? Given the ability of central and east European politicians to outdo the Vicar of Bray in changing policies and the emergence of indistinct centralist groupings this is not surprising. Hence, former communists can now support privatisation and market reform. As Chapter 2 showed, political stability is rarely as advanced as economic reform.

The divergence between economic gain and political stability is illustrated by opinion polls taken in early 1994 in Hungary prior to the general election which returned a socialist (former communist) government. Hungary, of course, is the central and east European country which to the general public would seem to have made the greatest progress towards a market economy, although recent economic indicators are showing a return to some bad old ways, particularly in the continuation of production even where external and internal markets have collapsed. The opinion poll conducted for the Economic and Social Research Council in the UK carried out by Modus in association with Gallup showed that 40 per cent of Hungarians who intended to vote Socialist said they now believed in the ideals of communism even if in practice it was not perfect. More worrying still, in the same poll most Hungarians felt the best time this century for them was under Kadar's communist regime, even although most Hungarians still supported a market economy although one modelled on Sweden rather than the United States.

A good example of where the political/economic bridge may effectively have been built is the Czech Republic, where a consistent set of policies has been presented over a number of years under a forceful leader. The political success of a speedy mass privatisation programme (voucher privatisation) in which large numbers of people participated seems to have provided reform with a momentum to which the political sophistication of the Czechs was equal, although, as Chapter 7 will show, even the Czechs appear discontented over the progress of democracy.

This was not initially the case in Russia, where the haphazard way in which the voucher privatisation programme was introduced was linked neither with perceived economic benefits nor with any concerted political support.

Another example of a successful bridge between economics and politics is Poland, where the 1993 election of a government of former Communists was regarded as the nightmare scenario for the country. In fact, the economic realities have been grasped readily and it is the very same former Communists who have presided over the introduction of mass privatisation, a 42.5 per cent debt-forgiveness in Poland's commercial debt, and a Stock Exchange which continued to run at record levels until late Spring 1994.

Nevertheless, even in Poland there is still substantial need for assistance in developing a permanent civil service independent of government and strengthening local government institutions.

A NEW MARSHALL PLAN WAS REJECTED

At the time that the EBRD was being founded and most of the technical assistance programmes were beginning to develop, there was considerable talk in the west of a Marshall Plan to aid the development of central and eastern Europe. The idea of this was taken from the plan to aid western Europe developed principally under the aegis of the United States after the Second World War. However, what most commentators thought of as the new Marshall Plan boiled down to little more than co-ordination of activities between donor agencies, harmonisation of political objectives and particularly the demands that should be placed on the use of the money, and, finally, the integration of assistance money with the private sector either as its develops locally or more likely through foreign, direct investment.

This idea was rejected for a number of reasons. First, western governments were frightened by the costs which were likely to be involved and the continuity of recession implied by continuing high interest rates. Second, there was already rivalry between the institutions producing the funds as to which should take the dominant position, and thirdly there was rivalry between individual governments as to what would be in it for them.

Attali, for example (1994) describes how George Bush proposed a G7-led initiative in 1989 based on individual G7 countries leading in the field of their own specialisation. Attali takes great pride in saying how, as host, France killed the idea largely because there was not enough in it for Europe, by which he appears substantially to have meant France. As a result, we got EBRD and the EU's PHARE and TACIS programmes neither of which have exercised a substantial degree of control over the western technical assistance effort as a whole.

It has taken four years to get any structure of co-ordination in place – this time at G24 level – but, as most of the institutions complain, the level of co-ordination is inadequate, there is duplication of effort, partial disclosure between institutions of programmes, and intense rivalry as to which should lead on the major, high-profile projects.

HOW EFFECTIVE HAS THE KNOW-HOW TRANSFER BEEN?

Given the imprecise, unco-ordinated and generalised objectives set by each funding source, it is difficult to measure their effectiveness overall in other than the most superficial of macro-economic terms. At the level of individual technical assistance projects, the situation is not much more precise.

In the case of the EU's PHARE and TACIS programmes, Sir Leon Brittan in his 1993 address to the European Parliament made great play that they relied on the east Europeans themselves to report back on the effectiveness of the programmes. Yet if the central and east Europeans are skilled enough to be able to provide in-depth critique of often complicated consultancy assignments why did they not undertake the assignment on their own in the first place? Some assistance programmes have put in measures of effectiveness. The UK Know How Fund, for example, starting from scratch hired a number of individual consultants whose role is to cover sectoral areas, helping the identification of projects and monitoring progress during the course of the project in order to act as the interface between the assistance agency and the government. It is not surprising, therefore, that in an informal series of questions which have been put over the past years to a number of recipients of assistance, the Know How Fund has come out as the one which the majority thinks achieves most for the money involved and has the highest level of effectiveness. This is notwithstanding the very small amount of money involved.

Perhaps, though, one of the key measures of effectiveness is in the responsiveness and flexibility of the programmes themselves.

Whilst there clearly is a need for an overall structure for any assistance programme, events in central and eastern Europe move so rapidly and needs change so quickly that assistance programmes need to be able to respond in like fashion. Most assistance programmes have difficulty with this sort of approach since they are nervous about having strict procedures for the disbursement of public funds. Smaller funds, such as the Know How Fund, have made flexibility of response a specific attribute. The larger funds have not, and it has not been unusual for consultants to receive invitations to bid on assignments where the terms of reference are irrelevant to the changed situation in the recipient country but the assignment still fits neatly into a pre-determined indicative programme.

USE OF CONSULTANTS HAS BEEN NAIVE

Surprisingly, perhaps, many of the funding agencies are not particularly sophisticated or skilled in using the principal means of delivering the assistance – consultants. There seems to be a presumption that consultants are in it for as much as they can get in fees in the short term, an attitude similar to that examined later in relation to multinationals and their relationship with the funding agencies. Such an attitude totally ignores the investment made by consultants in the region which, for example in at least one case had given rise to over 1,000 partners and staff of the firm resident in the region by early 1994.

Many institutions seem to see consultants as one generic group over which they can impose uniform conditions regardless of whether the assignment can be conducted by a lone individual or requires the back-up and support of one of the major consulting firms. Indeed, this hostility towards the big consulting firms, coupled in some cases with a less than clear transparency in the selection of firms to appear on tender lists, produces often a recipe for disaster. Stories in relation to the EU of assignments being 'pre-won', ie before being advertised, after strong country pressure even at Council of Ministers level, are too numerous to be apocryphal.

Sir Leon Brittan in his 1993 speech to the European Parliament said that 'the need to rely too heavily on consultants has caused resentment in the countries of central and eastern Europe because of the costs involved and the transitory nature of their involvement'. This reflects concern in eastern Europe for a phenomenon known as 'consultancy tourism' where consultants, often from small firms with no long-term interest in the countries concerned and certainly with none of their own money put into those countries, zip in and out to undertake studies with little implementation and often questionable quality.

There is no doubt that the EU as a funder of these firms is regarded as the worst offender in this respect, in effectively encouraging this practice to continue. At a conference in Brussels in 1994 to a distinguished audience of European management, legal, engineering and technical consultants, a senior PHARE and TACIS official announced that he did not need any of the consultancies represented in the room, that he could always find cheaper firms in southern Europe which would still meet minimum quality standards, and that the reason the EU wished to see the plane ticket stubs of consultants (however synonymous their firms were with 'integrity') was because the EU did not trust them and believed they might 'be on the beach in Portugal when [they] said they were working in Russia'.

In a European context, 'consultancy tourism' has, therefore, arisen as a natural result of the EU's own prejudices and the scope of the assignments it sets. For example, it has been made quite clear that the EU does not recognise the existence of centres of excellence and is committed to spreading the work, even if that means removing from a short list the next time around a large firm which has handled several projects and built up experience. 'A firm, even if it is capable, that has already received a certain number of contracts may not appear on future lists for some time'; and that is a direct quote from Peter Kalbe, the head of Phare and Tacis Information Services (*Management Consulting International*, June/July 1993, 3).

Such unsophisticated and naive attitudes towards consultants is depriving eastern Europe of the best teams for the job and leads to the consultancy tourism trap set out in Figure 3.1.

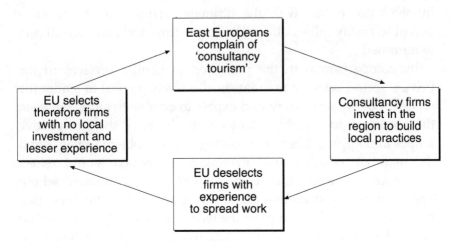

Figure 3.1 *The 'consultancy tourism' trap*

PROJECT DEFINITION COULD BE IMPROVED[1]

A further issue arises in connection with the way in which projects are defined. In many cases the need for a particular service has been identified and mutually accepted by the local government and the funding institution. The funding institution then defines the project by drafting terms of reference, running to many pages, in which it estimates the time and the price for the work. Both figures may be made known when invitations to bid are announced.

This approach leads to extremely time-consuming preparation of tenders on the part of the bidders, which may take the form of a detailed critique of the terms of reference (and probably a bid in excess of the sum said to be appropriate by the agency) but

---

[1] I am grateful for British Invisibles' Central and East European panel for these comments.

involves no contact with the ultimate recipient of the services except to clarify information. The scope, time and price are all pre-determined.

By comparison with the provision of similar services in the private sector, even if a mandate is effectively put out to tender the recipient of the services would expect to be able to judge between the tenderers to a large extent on the basis of their respective scopes and approaches to the solving of the problem in hand, and the mandate which would eventually be issued would reflect discussions between the recipient and the practitioner whose approach was considered the most appropriate. The time that would be required to complete the work, and its cost, would not be decided until a clear idea of what would be entailed had been established.

A great deal of unnecessary work is, therefore, undertaken by the agency concerned, and, in particular, by bidders, as a result of attempts to provide very detailed terms of reference for particular services before the consortium which would provide the services, or the ultimate recipient of those services, have had a chance to discuss what should be involved. If the agencies were to adopt a less rigid approach to the way in which proposals have to be presented, the bidders could produce much more imaginative proposals which would be likely to be much more useful to the agencies and the recipient governments or institutions. Private sector experience suggests that, in circumstances of this kind, the bidders would effectively be giving some free advice as part of their proposals and that by comparing and contrasting the different proposals received the recipient is much more likely to be able to use the proposal as a means of defining more clearly the work that it requires.

WHO BENEFITS?

The question of for whose benefit the assistance is intended may seem facetious but follows from the preceding discussion and the inevitable way in which discussion of technical assistance always focuses on the manner of delivery rather than the benefit to the recipient. This is not primarily dictated by the self-interest of writers who are also consultants. It stems from two principal causes.

First, the specific objectives of programmes and of individual assignments are often so imprecise that nothing much can be gained from a sterile argument about effectiveness.

Second, the process of delivering the projects is so needlessly bureaucratic, so inconvenient and so seemingly designed to satisfy internal western regulations rather than the needs of the recipients, that it cannot fail to provoke comment.

WHAT IS REQUIRED AND WHERE ARE WE NOW?

In helping to measure effectiveness, the development of the recipient countries needs to be put into perspective. The needs of the recipient countries, and therefore of the funding agencies, clearly change over time. Broadly these needs can be divided into four phases. Although in this model the phases are expected to be consecutive, it is clear that individual sectors within an economy may move at different rates.

The model is illustrated in Figure 3.2 below.

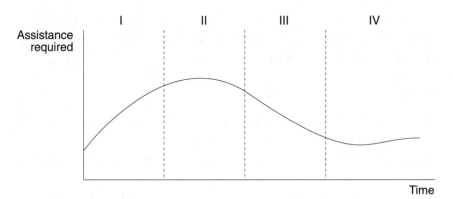

Figure 3.2 *Model of development*

Phase I

In Phase I, economic reform has only just commenced. Governments are likely to be in close discussion with the IMF, World Bank and other lenders as to the amount of loans required and conversely the programme of economic reforms which will be required.

In this phase, technical assistance is most effectively targeted at macro-economic reviews, studies of socio-economic implications, and some initial drafting of new legislation (including legislation to encourage inward investment). There is also likely to be an essential need for assistance in ensuring statistical information can be provided quickly and accurately. Consideration will be required at this stage usually of the extent to which fiscal and monetary policy can be changed.

In Poland, for example, this phase lasted until the introduction of the short, sharp shock reforms. In Russia, elements of this phase are still continuing.

Technical assistance ought also to be targeted in this phase at providing assistance in the design of appropriate political structures, preparation for elections, development of a permanent civil service and other public sector reform. At the same time, it needs to focus on the social assistance which is going to be required to deal with unemployment, whether that be social security support or incentives to develop small service businesses, or some other form of social safety net.

Phase II

Phase II will usually see the first major steps to reform and some of the harshest economic measures. Technical assistance and loans ought, therefore, to be directed towards ensuring that this phase is short and effective.

Price reform, banking reform, privatisation and fiscal reform all need to be pushed through. In the case of privatisation, for example, this is the period of pilot privatisations designed to demonstrate the success of privatisation as a concept.

In tandem with these reforms there is usually regulatory reform in the law, accounting and financial institutions. There is also the restructuring of government departments and the creation of new organisations such as inward investment agencies, privatisation agencies, etc.

In order to demonstrate progress to the voters, this is also the time for major infrastructure projects in energy development, telecommunications, etc.

Russia, Kazakhstan, Romania and Bulgaria tend to fall into this stage in mid-1994.

Political assistance is essential in this phase to confirming the existence of a non-partisan, professional civil service as changes of government may occur frequently in response to voter concerns over the economic reforms. Social assistance needs to be provided in overhauling the state benefits and pensions set-up and ensuring that the social safety net is appropriately targeted.

Phase III

Phase III marks the success or failure of the reform programme as the first real effects of reform are felt throughout the economy.

If the buy-in of the voters has been obtained in Phase II, measures such as full-scale privatisation, restructuring and positive trade measures will occur. Individual companies, newly privatised, now begin to act independently. Companies require restructuring and new funds and decisions need to be made about residual State holdings in industry. Stock Exchanges emerge and regulations, such as investor protection legislation, are required.

Poland and Hungary are substantially in this phase in mid-1994.

Political assistance is probably best concentrated at this stage in achieving strong local government, while social assistance is likely to be targeted towards ensuring that a free job market works in practice.

Phase IV

Phase IV is an open-ended phase. Its duration and the amount of money required depend on the extent to which the reforms of Phases I – III have really taken hold and not been simply superficial. Further work in developing capital markets, in dealing with bankruptcies and in developing national budgeting is likely to be required.

Arguably, the Czech Republic has just begun to enter this phase.

Technical assistance and other aid needs to recognise these phases to ensure that the funding matches the requirements and can exercise positive influence on the direction of the reform process.

A LEVEL OF CO-ORDINATION IS REQUIRED

Such models are usually seen as somewhat simplistic and unflexible in relation to the complexities within emerging economies. This, of course, is to some extent quite true. However, agreement between the agencies on such a framework would at least provide a series of benchmarks and objectives against which the progress and effectiveness could be judged and more accurately correlated against reform at a wide range of levels.

Naturally, this implies a greater level of co-ordination between funding agencies than we have so far seen. EBRD under Attali, for example, was usually trying to act one step ahead of a country's position on the curve. The EU were, as a result of the length of their planning process, often some way behind. Smaller funds, such as the Know How Fund, were able to be flexible and responsive and, therefore, generally be in the right place at the right time.

It also implies that there is sufficient data produced on a timely basis to enable a country's economic situation to be assessed accurately and that agreement could be reached amongst economists on the interpretation of the data in order to assess a country's economic development.

Co-ordination of the first type has so far eluded us in providing technical assistance to central and eastern Europe. Agreement between economists is a Holy Grail which many will continue to search for in vain for many years to come.

THE WORLD BANK

The institution which comes closest to following such a model of central and eastern Europe is the World Bank. Perhaps this is not surprising in view of the length of time the World Bank has been in this type of business compared with the other funding agencies involved in the region. Linked closely with the IMF and other Washington-based institutions, the World Bank has had a unique picture of the interplay between east and west at the highest levels.

Its serious commitment to the area cannot be doubted and is reflected in its internal structure and the creation of a separate unit to deal with the problems. In addition, its programmes are generally well thought out and comprehensive, even though they take little input from outside sources in the field when compiling them.

Yet even the World Bank has not taken the leading role in co-ordinating assistance and has shown itself to be prepared to fight its own corner to try to maintain some form of hegemony in a fractured, technical assistance establishment.

CONCLUSIONS

The effectiveness of technical assistance cannot ultimately be measured in a vacuum. Its effectiveness can best be measured by the extent to which it has contributed to the overall direction of change which all the stakeholders in the region – aid, lenders, private investors, local government, technical assistance programmes, etc – are trying to achieve. Measured in these terms, technical assistance programmes have not been unqualified successes.

The reasons for this are set out throughout this chapter and Chapter 2, but it is worth summarising the main points.

1. With some exceptions, there cannot really be said to have been a common plan to which technical assistance providers could have signed up. The conditionality applying to funds differs quite markedly between agencies. Local governments across the regions have different objectives and often quite radically-different economic programmes.

2. Within such common direction as exists, the appropriateness and relevance of some technical assistance programmes to local government policy and the practical situation in the country must be questioned. This comes back to the appropriateness of the assistance to the position of the country on the curve set out in Figure 3.2 above.

3. The bulk of technical assistance has been directed to the economic infrastructure, with insufficient attention paid to the political and social requirements of the country.

4. A year is a very long time in central and eastern Europe and developments have often moved faster than the assistance programmes' internal planning procedures. Speed and flexibility have not been hallmarks of the programmes.

5. The level of real co-ordination between agencies has been abysmal and has rarely moved beyond general discussion of project pipelines. This has resulted in overlaps, wasted effort and unfocused activity.

6. The rivalry between agencies as to which should take the lead has diverted efforts into a fruitless battle only of interest to the agencies concerned.

7. The level of bureaucracy in accessing the funds has been unacceptable. For example, it is not unusual for contract negotiations following the award of a project to take over three months to complete before the project can begin.

8. The use of the main resource for delivering assignments – consultants – has been naive and inflexible and too hedged with western political concerns.

Given that central and eastern Europe was an unprecedented situation, is it fair to criticise the agencies for reacting in this way, or in other words, am I expecting too much of them?

In the first place, the political rhetoric of the time was based on George Bush's declaration of a 'new world order'. It does not seem to me to be unfair to have looked for some proof of the order's existence in a wider vision of dealing with central and eastern Europe above individual, national self-interests.

Second, central and eastern Europe was not entirely unique. Aid and assistance programmes had been undertaken in, for example, Africa during previous decades by the international community. The lessons which should have been learnt from this experience clearly were not. For these reasons we could have expected more and should expect more when the same challenge arises in relation to South-east Asia and China, or even once more in Africa.

4

The Return to the Private Sector

One of the key reforms on which technical assistance funds have been spent is 'privatisation'. What do we mean by privatisation? Is the mechanistic definition, heard frequently in central and eastern Europe, that it is about the transfer of more than 50% of the ownership of a business from the public sector into private hands, adequate? After all, who is kidding whom that any real change has occurred in this process if management remains the same and the State continues to subsidise the business either directly or through cheap loans from State-controlled banks? Privatisation surely means more than changing the name on a share certificate. Does it not imply a willingness, amongst other things, to remove or significantly diminish State assistance and allow businesses, where necessary, to be put into liquidation with potentially consequent social costs?

Is it then a deeply political process in which the principal aim is to shift the balance between the collective and the individual in society firmly in the direction of the latter? In other words, is privatisation more about politics, or more about economics?

These questions may seem naive, in that privatisation is clearly a complex web of political, economic and social engineering. The questions are relevant, however, in looking at the way in which privatisation programmes have been developed in central and eastern Europe, and in setting the objectives of the programmes against which success can be measured.

WHY PRIVATISE?

Why have the countries of central and eastern Europe embarked on privatisation programmes? At the risk of cynicism, one key answer is because they were told to do so by the IMF, the World Bank and by the other creditor institutions which had lent them substantial sums of money to stave off increasing trends toward national bankruptcy. But this raises another question. How were these western institutions so confident in the efficacy of privatisation when their own experience of it was, in reality, quite minimal? What was put forward with certainty as a proven, economic path to success was in fact an experiment on the scale of which no one had ever operated before, and on a scale from which most western governments would have shrunk from trying to introduce in their own countries.

In the UK, the pioneer of this experiment, more than ten years of keen privatisation had resulted in only some 40 companies being transferred to the private sector, although the considerable debate which occurred in the early 1980s in the UK had covered many of the issues subsequently to arise, including the concept of voucher privatisation. The UK experience had principally been in the development of share issues to the public for which a professional combination of merchant bank, accountant and lawyer became the norm.

As even *Le Monde* admitted, this experience, not only of privatisation itself but also of efficient and effective multi-disciplinary co-operation in developing the process, could not be matched by continental European countries where privatisation had been virtually non-existent, and where professional experience had principally been orientated towards the buying and selling of companies between trade investors.

In these circumstances, it is even more incredible that some of the donor agencies failed to recognise the centre of European excellence which had emerged in the UK and insisted, for their own internal, political reasons, in spreading the privatisation work to consultants from countries which had even less experience and understanding of privatisation than the central and east Europeans themselves.

Another surprising feature has been the virtual absence of any western opposition to the selling of wholesale privatisation, even amongst socialist politicians and economists.

Given the increasingly lukewarm attitude of the British public to privatisation as it came to include further utilities, railways, prisons, etc and the identical comments raised in the UK, (even by former Tory Prime Ministers) and in central and eastern Europe about the family silver being sold off too cheaply, it is even more surprising how feeble the debate has been about the merits of a programme on which considerable amounts of money have been spent and on which considerable hopes were, and still are, pinned.

Perhaps some of the explanation lies in the fact that the most high-profile privatisation programmes in central and eastern Europe have been mass privatisation programmes, whereby substantial tranches of industry have been privatised at a stroke by effectively being given away (or sold at a low price) to the people at large. Left-of-centre governments (including former communists) in Poland and Hungary have had no difficulty in supporting such privatisation programmes.

WHAT TYPE OF PRIVATISATION?

There have been essentially four types of privatisation. These are set out in Table 4.1 and are described further below. The key feature of this is just how varied the privatisation methods have been in all of the major countries in the region. One of the earliest messages given to these countries at the beginning of the privatisation process was that one method was unlikely to be effective and that options needed to be kept open so that process and company could more adequately be matched.

Table 4.1 *Privatisation methods*

Method	Countries
Mass privatisation	Czech Republic, Slovakia, Hungary, Poland, Romania, Bulgaria, Latvia, Lithuania, Estonia, Russia, Ukraine, Kazakhstan, Belarus, Slovenia
Sectoral privatisation	Poland, Hungary, Bulgaria
Individual privatisations	All countries
• trade sale	
• public offers	
• MBO/employees	
Small-scale privatisation	All countries

Mass Privatisation

Probably the most famous privatisation process has been mass privatisation. The term mass privatisation conceals a number of methods of privatisation, but the common objective of them all has been the rapid transfer of ownership in large numbers of enterprises to the private sector, usually for minimal or even no cost where the transfer is to the domestic population at large and with minimal, or even no, prior restructuring.

The first, and undoubtedly most successful, mass privatisation programme has been the Czech and Slovak voucher privatisation scheme in which the local population were eligible to purchase vouchers at an attractive price, these vouchers being then exchanged through a series of bidding rounds for shares in companies. This could be done either directly or via intermediary investment funds set up in the private sector. This process has taken place over a number of years and in two main waves. It has been accompanied subsequently by the development of share trading mechanisms which have given Prague the only successful, paperless, share trading system in Europe and, inevitably, by regulation of the market. Its success can be measured in the number of people (some eight million) who participated and therefore felt part of the reform process in a more dynamic way.

However, as Table 4.2 below sets out, although the Czech and Slovak schemes formed the spur to the development of other mass privatisation schemes elsewhere, its features have not been copied wholesale and many schemes are radically different. For ease of presentation, the programmes in Poland, Hungary, Czech Republic and Russia have been selected although, as Table 4.1 above showed, the phenomenon is more widespread.

Sector Privatisation

Sector privatisations are in many ways designed to establish the best methods of privatisation within a key sector in order to prevent its piecemeal disposal and to try to retain maximum value for the State in the sector as a whole. In this respect, sectoral privatisations are often portrayed as being once-in-a-lifetime sales of whole sectors creating more intense international competition

Table 4.2 *Mass privatisation methods*

Specific features	Czech Republic	Hungary	Poland	Russia
Principal method	Vouchers	Cheap loans	Shares in intermediary funds	Vouchers
General features	Vouchers issued for KCR 1000 1st and 2nd wave. All citizens over 18 entitled to participate. Complex series of bidding processes to convert vouchers into shares. Effected either directly or via private investment funds acting as intermediaries.	Assistance provided in the direct purchase of shares by means of interest-free loans repayable over 5 years. All citizens over 18 eligible.	Shares will be distributed through National Investment Funds. All citizens over 18 eligible. Cost US$15. Number of shares received for this price depends on subscription to funds.	Vouchers issued for free. All citizens over 18 entitled to participate Vouchers converted into shares through auction process or through private invest-ment funds.
Number of companies included	1,804	Up to 70	At least 400	Over 5,000
Value of companies included	US$8.75 billion	Not yet known (280.6 billion HUF)	Not yet known (60,000 billion Zloty)	Not yet known
Restrictions on subsequent disposal of shares	No	Yes	No	No
Extent to which controlled or market-driven	Market-driven	Controlled	Controlled	Market-driven
Participation of foreign investors	In parallel	In parallel	In parallel	Direct or in parallel
Development of investor protection measures	High	Medium	High	Low
Number of people participating	8.5 million	Not yet known	Not yet known	†
Funded by	KHF	KHF	KHF	IFC/KHF

Key

† Vouchers were issued to approximately 100 million people

and, therefore, higher sales prices. Such an approach usually involves a review of all major companies within the sector, including some benchmarking of the companies with international competitors as well as benchmarking the sector as a whole as one, for example, of key or strategic interest to the country. By looking at all companies within the sector at once, individual governments are likely to be able to assess a more realistic view of value and to be able to exert more pressure on investors in negotiation to ensure that the 'dogs' are disposed of in a package with the 'stars'.

However, as the Polish sectoral programme showed, the choice of sectors is crucial. Some sectors although important domestically, may not be of interest to foreign investors or may be sectors where internationally there is little cross-border activity. The choice of sectors, therefore, needs to be integrated into foreign investment promotion plans as a whole and to effective, alternative, financing routes where they are of domestic interest only.

Individual Privatisations

There are a number of different variants within this grouping. At one end of the scale has been the typical British privatisation – the public issue of shares. Examples of this include five pilot enterprises in Poland and the regional Romanian brewery in Cluj – Ursus. For governments, such privatisations have been ideal testing grounds for seeing in detail how the privatisation process works. However, within the companies themselves there are indications that the individual spot lights under which the privatisations occurred were a little too revealing and heightened, rather than alleviated, management fears over continuity and worker fears over employment.

For the new shareholders, such privatisations were often their first direct experience of capitalism. In Romania this had rather unexpected results. Following the successful privatisation of the Ursus brewery, Cluj was selected by a company called Caritas as the main base for a pyramid banking scam – the biggest scam in Romania and, indeed, in central Europe. The choice of Cluj seems not to have been an accident. Bitten by the bug of legitimate capitalism, the citizens of Cluj were all too prepared to be bitten by its unacceptable face too.

Often, as indeed in the case of Ursus, public share issues are coupled with a sale of part of the shares to a trade investor in order to improve investment and management.

Such individual privatisations are usually based on a formal legal process where the enterprise is first transformed from a socialist enterprise into a recognisably corporate form, the shares of which are then fully or partially sold. In some cases, as in Poland for example, a liquidation method has been developed where, effectively, the assets of the former socialist enterprise are sold to a new company owned by the intended shareholders.

Other methods of individual privatisations include management buy-outs and employee leveraged buy-outs. In Hungary, for example, the first privatisations were spontaneous privatisations where businesses were sold to existing management. The Russian privatisation programme also envisages significant ownership by employees and management.

So far, there have been few examples of hostile bids from foreign investors, although in theory this is possible at least in Hungary. However, effective privatisations have been created for some time by the hive-down of parts of businesses to new joint venture companies.

Small-scale Privatisation

Almost all central and east European countries have embarked on small-scale privatisation programmes. These have been directed at selling off to the local population small businesses such as restaurants and shops. This has usually been done through public auctions.

WHAT ARE THE OBJECTIVES?

There are a number of diverse objectives which each of these privatisation approaches illustrate. These objectives are not necessarily shared by all approaches but they do provide a framework at least for measuring the effectiveness of privatisation against the aims of that particular programme.

Political objectives

- To transfer ownership to the private sector as widely as possible and reduce State interference.

- To encourage commitment to reform.

- To re-orientate the balance of society.

- To move to a market-led economy.

Macro-economic objectives

- To reduce State obligations and control.

- To cut the budget deficit.

- To increase State revenues from privatisation sales.

- To provide domestic and international competitiveness.

- To provide sustainable growth.

Micro-economic objectives

- Lower personal and corporate taxes.

- Corporate efficiency.

- Profitability.

- Sustainable employment.

External objectives

- To meet IMF and creditor programmes.

- To reduce borrowing.

THE EMPHASIS OF THE VARIOUS PRIVATISATION METHODS

Mass privatisation

The mass privatisation programmes have to a large extent been directed in the first instance towards satisfying political objectives. In the case of the Czech Republic (and the Slovak 'first wave') it was clear that the overriding imperative was a political statement of the sort of market economy Vaclav Klaus, its then finance minister, wanted to see achieved in the shortest time. As was argued in Chapter 3, the success of this strategy appears to have brought a greater level of economic and political stability to the Czech Republic. Clearly, from an economic point of view, there were also enormous benefits but these were secondary.

One indication of this is that the selection process for admitting an enterprise to the privatisation programme in the Czech Republic envisaged no substantial restructuring before privatisation, whereas in Poland more stringent criteria have been set which would favour companies which have undertaken at least some level of restructuring.

In its initial concept, the Polish mass privatisation programme was also directed towards achieving immediate political aims. However, the protracted political controversy surrounding it and the frequent change of governments have dissipated the political impact. The main objective is, therefore, now arguably an economic one in contributing to sustainable economic reform.

The Russian privatisation programme, like the Czech, was also aimed at achieving political objectives. The first major mass auction – in St. Petersburg – was rushed through at a time when President Yeltsin was at a nadir in his relationship with the conservative parliament, to try to boost the reform process and buy-in the participation of the people. Economic benefit has not really been felt, despite a large number of companies being privatised by early 1994, since little restructuring had taken place. The prostitutes of Perm, who at one time were reported as accepting only privatisation vouchers for their services, must wonder what economic benefit they now have.

In the Czech Republic and Poland, initial fears by management that mass privatisation would lead to their replacement did not result in effective blocking tactics or substantial distortions in the market. Regulation and control over the process were tighter. But the enthusiastic commitment of the population at large also provided significant momentum. In Russia, however, this was not always the case.

A scandal arose during 1994 in respect of the Gorky Automobile Works (GAZ), Russia, makers of the Chaika limousine: a conservative management seems to have been intent on preventing mass privatisation having any real micro-economic effect, particularly in changing management and business practices. In this case, the management were accused of illegally abusing the voucher privatisation programme by using proxies to acquire sufficient vouchers to give them a sizeable block of shares in the privatised GAZ. This was despite probable technical bankruptcy and a continuing production-led mentality which had some 45,000 trucks sitting as unsold, completed product (*Independent*, 17 March 1994).

Clearly, privatisation cannot be seen as successful in this context if a change of name on the share certificate is as far as it goes. Other changes must also occur to the privatised companies and to the economic environment in which they operate.

Sectoral privatisation

In contrast the clear emphasis of sectoral privatisation has been principally to achieve macro-economic objectives. The idea of looking at sectors as a whole has been to take drastic action, where necessary, to reform inefficient and costly sectors where there was possibility for competitiveness and sustainable growth, and to maximise State returns.

In this respect, some sectors are clearly more successful than others. However, too often the measure of success for sectoral privatisation has been the volume of cash proceeds which can be generated from subsequent sales of companies to foreign investors. The Poles themselves point to the pulp and paper, detergents and brewing sectors as examples of this, while downplaying those sectors such as food and clothing where equally successful privatisations may occur but with only domestic investors.

Individual privatisations

The diversity of privatisation methods within the heading of individual privatisations has ensured that there is a corresponding diversity of objectives which are achieved. Most of these have been economic in character, however, and many individual privatisations have run into considerable local political difficulties.

An example of this, though from early in the privatisation process, is the case of HungarHotels in Hungary (Howell, 1991 (a)).

THE CASE OF HUNGARHOTELS

Under then Hungarian Law (The Transformation Act) an asset valuation was undertaken of HungarHotels in order to establish a balance sheet for the corporation. This valuation was an estimation of the replacement cost of the assets. The instincts of the Hungarian government in drafting the Transformation Law had been to use the method of valuation with which they were most comfortable, rather than the method which commercially may have been more appropriate.

The result of this valuation showed an overall gross asset valuation of approximately US$290 million (HuF 18.9bn) and a net asset valuation of approximately US$170 million (HuF11bn).

Following this valuation a Swedish corporation, Quintus, purchased a 50 per cent interest in the new HungarHotels corporation for US$87 million (HuF5.7 bn).

This transaction attracted much attention in Hungary in the context of what was then a developing, political campaign for the first, free, Hungarian general elections. The then Minister of Trade, Tamas Beck, had been a leading critic of the deal and of the sale of national assets at what he perceived as 'bargain rates' by comparing the market sale price with the asset valuation.

As a result, the Hungarian authorities referred the sale to Quintus to the Hungarian Supreme Court and a decision was eventually made to reverse the transaction on technical grounds. There can be no doubt that this was a highly political issue.

The fundamental problem was that the Hungarian authorities failed to understand the difference between an asset valuation and a business valuation. The asset valuation, under Hungarian law, made no pretence at being a market value of the corporation as a whole, which would need to take account of liabilities and future cash flows. Yet, from a political perspective, it was the asset valuation that confirmed the belief that there should have been a higher value for Hungarian national assets than was justified by what the market would in fact pay.

Indeed, a subsequent business valuation of HungarHotels based on earnings was conducted as a limited scope exercise for HungarHotel's management. This showed a value in the region of US$120.90m (HuF8.6bn) representing inflation and poor results expected from many of the hotels.

In the light of this, it is difficult to see why, on business grounds, Quintus's valuation of its intended share of HungarHotels when grossed up for the whole company was not seen as a good offer.

Many countries may argue that such views of privatisation were characteristic of an earlier phase of reform and that they are not widely held now. To some extent that may be true. However, views similar to that of Tamas Beck are still current in the West amongst left-of-centre groups challenging privatisation in their own countries, and re-emerge from time to time even in central Europe itself.

THE MAJOR PROBLEMS

There are essentially three major areas which still have to be managed in respect of privatisation in central and eastern Europe. These are:

- Post-privatisation success and continuing the momentum.

- Secondary trading markets and the issues of regulations.

- The interaction with foreign investment.

These are briefly examined below.

POST-PRIVATISATION SUCCESS

Momentum

The speed with which privatisation, particularly mass privatisation, has taken place has ensured a high profile for the process and higher expectations that noticeable, positive change would emerge. In some cases these expectations were based on the belief that the companies selected for privatisation would survive and prosper. In other cases, expectations were based on improbably high returns promised by fund managers acting as intermediaries.

In the case of mass privatisation programmes the momentum has been more difficult to sustain, as post-privatisation consolidation has been seen inevitably as an anti-climax after the razzmatazz generated by the privatisation itself. The momentum, however, needs to be continued through the development of effective and accessible secondary markets.

Similarly, the momentum for individual privatisations has been extraordinarily difficult to maintain because of the slower pace at which the privatisations proceed and the expense of privatising individual companies. As we have already seen, the momentum may also be halted by anti-foreign investor feeling aimed at perceived low sale prices and subsequent changes in government policy.

Success

Post-privatisation success is even more unpredictable. Most mass privatisation programmes have been based on minimal screening of the companies entering the programme, little prior restructuring and no guarantees as to their survivability. Some of the companies may have technically been bankrupt at the time of privatisation and others may subsequently have become so. In the case of individual privatisation the selection process has usually been more rigorous and the presence of consultants on-site during the privatisation has often led to the identification of restructuring needs and sometimes to restructuring projects.

Since post-privatisation success is linked to the requirements of the business, privatisation in itself is unlikely to lead to management changes, improved performance, or necessarily the injection of new money into the business. Yet to restructure first and privatise second would have significantly eroded the political momentum to reform overall. The question of whether privatisation is primarily political or economic is again relevant.

In terms of expectations, the post-privatisation phase is the most difficult for governments to manage since they have usually withdrawn from direct or overt involvement with the companies themselves and may be politically hostile to interventionist moves. Dissatisfaction with this phase is often a major contributor to the political backlash which emerges and sweeps former communists back into power.

In this respect, few countries have yet fully been prepared to allow newly-privatised companies or even residual State companies to be exposed fully to the rigours of the market. Few bankruptcies have taken place despite legislation to allow them. Indeed, even in the Czech Republic there appears to have been a greater management of the process of post-privatisation restructuring to prevent a political fall-out from a rapid rise in unemployment than expected.

Secondary trading markets

In some countries, for example Hungary and Poland, Stock Markets were already in existence prior to the implementation of mass privatisation. In Poland, for example, the Warsaw Bourse in early 1994 had been trading in the shares of twenty-three companies at levels rivalling the volume of daily trading on the New York Stock Exchange. An increase in value of some 700 per cent during 1993 on the Exchange indicated 'transaction fever', which eventually produced the April crash as investors recognised for the first time that share prices could go down as well as up. The Czech Exchange, by contrast, was created on the back of the mass privatisation programme. Although having a higher capitalisation than the Warsaw Bourse, the levels of trading have been more reflective of company values.

Whether Stock Exchanges pre-date mass privatisation programmes or not, the impact of the programmes on the need for effective and accessible secondary market mechanisms needs to be seen as part-and-parcel of the privatisation programme. This has not always been the case even with mass privatisation programmes, and has certainly not been the case with a number of individual privatisations even where they have involved issues of shares to the public.

Allied to this is the need for regulation of the way in which the secondary markets will operate, especially in respect of ethical guidelines and investor protection legislation. Such legislation not only provides comfort for local investors and prevents the politically damaging spectacle of scandal, it also encourages foreign investment into the markets.

The interaction with foreign investment

For most central and east European companies, as we shall later see, direct foreign investment has been seen as virtually the only access route to new capital, new technology and new management.

Yet foreign investors have often had a love-hate relationship with privatisation and the opportunities it could bring.

On the one hand, it was privatisation which was likely to release the specific opportunities in State companies which were going to be of most interest and convey most strategic advantage. On the other hand, the process by which the foreign investor became involved was often fraught. Unrealistic local expectations over value, bureaucratic delays, political considerations, the length of time taken to complete the deal, and enforced international competitive tender all contributed to the erosion of competitive advantage potentially inherent in the transaction.

Coupled with legal uncertainties as to ownership of assets, warranties for post-environmental liabilities, and access to open competition on the domestic markets, these factors often deterred companies from bidding as part of the privatisation process.

In the case of one particularly high-value investment in Poland, for example, the completion of the transaction was dragged out over a number of months simply because there was no one on the Polish government side willing to accept the cheque for the European company's investment. Negotiations were hampered by frequent changes of government, which resulted in changes in senior civil servants as well.

CONCLUSIONS

Despite the need to manage these three areas, the privatisation process in central Europe must surely be seen as a success when measured by the political objectives of transferring State ownership of industry and commerce to the private sector. By the end of 1993 the percentage of GDP generated from the private sector in the three, principal, central European countries was as shown in Table 4.3 below:

Table 4.3 *Percentage of GDP originating in the private sector as at 31 December 1993*

Country	Percentage
Poland	50
Hungary	39
Czech Republic	44

Source: *Various*

Of course, all these countries did not start from the same base. Poland, for example, had had a high, private sector GDP component for many years representing the fact that Polish agriculture had not been collectivised, but the achievement is none the less creditable.

In the case of the rest of eastern Europe and particularly Russia, the effectiveness of privatisation even from a political point of view is still too close to call. In the minds of the people on the streets, the risk must be that, unless accompanied by other reforms, it will be seen not only as ineffective but also as irrelevant. As those reforms must include potentially damaging restructuring of companies, the political dilemma is obvious.

From an economic point of view, the success of privatisation is more difficult to assess. There was not, for example, the same emphasis on privatisation reducing the public sector need for borrowing as there was in the UK. Nevertheless, there were some expectations in terms of sales proceeds. In fact, income from privatisation sales has not been significant.

Ultimately, the success of privatisation will need to be judged by its contribution to the achievement overall of a successful market economy. Its greatest success will be in those countries where the commitment to overall reform is great and where it does not stand as an island of reform isolated from a still largely unchanged State sector. Its failure will be where it is a superficial change to show commitment to reform for other ends but with no underlying reform taking place.

CASE STUDIES

By way of example, three privatisations have been selected as short case studies. These are:

1. The privatisation of Ursus brewery in Romania.

2. The sectoral privatisation of the Polish meat industry.

3. The Czech voucher privatisation programme.

Ursus S.A. Cluj, Romania

The brewery of Ursus is based in the Transylvanian city of Cluj. It is one of a number of regional breweries in Romania but has a geographical, strategic advantage in its location near to the Hungarian border and to potential foreign export markets. Like all Romanian breweries, it lacked capital investment and new brewing technology. However, it had a youthful and forward-looking management eager to experiment with privatisation.

Ursus was selected as one of the first pilot privatisations in Romania funded by the Know How Fund and was the first public issue of shares to occur in Romania. The privatisation was carried out by a team of UK bankers, lawyers, public relations consultants and accountants, including Ernst & Young.

Although there was no established secondary market mechanism for trading the shares eventually issued to the public and no regulations, the share prospectus which was issued followed broadly EU requirements. Being the first public issue of shares in Romania, there was no established mechanism for advertising the prospectus or for distributing share applications and processing the results.

In the period of preparation for offer, the management of the company was exposed to a level of questioning on historical, current and future operations to which they had not been exposed before. After all, if there is one key rule of pilot privatisations it is that, at any cost, they must be seen to be successful. As a result, the management of the brewery obtained a clear picture that its future needs were not going to be satisfied solely through the issue of shares to the public and that a foreign, strategic partner would be required.

As with other privatisations in central and eastern Europe, the valuation of the business and the determination of the share price were the subject of considerable discussion in the face of unrealistic Romanian expectations. Similarly, it was difficult for the Romanian authorities to accept that the level of disclosure required in the prospectus, especially in relation to risks, should be as stringent and as comprehensive as proposed by the advisers.

Nevertheless, an office price having been set, the shares amounting to 51 per cent of the equity were sold through the branches of the Romanian Development Bank, which maintained special 'share windows' in its branches to facilitate the sales and provide additional information. The sale was accompanied by appropriate advertising and PR.

In the end, the full 51 per cent was sold, thus privatising the company. In addition, a sale was also arranged for the remaining 49 per cent to the German brewer, Brau und Brunnen. Subsequent to privatisation, the value of the company's shares increased dramatically, partially as a result of inflation, but largely because of the association with an investment by the foreign investor.

At one level, therefore, the privatisation of Ursus was a success and it showed very clearly that public share issues could be made to work even in an environment with a relatively under-developed, financial infrastructure. However, it also has shown that such privatisations can have little effect on the whole reform process unless they are followed up by rapid commitment to extend reform at a quick pace. Romania's commitment to reform, then as now, was faltering and the privatisation was opposed in some quarters. Laws necessary for the long-term success of the company and for the continuing enthusiasm of the shareholders remained in draft, including the nature of the secondary trading allowed in Ursus's shares.

The Polish meat sector

Ernst & Young were retained by the Polish government to provide a privatisation strategy in respect of the Polish meat sector. Unlike pulp and paper, chemicals, etc the meat sector in Europe is characterised by little, extensive cross-border ownership and by a predominance of small, family-owned companies. From the point of view of foreign investment, the sector was unlikely to be seen as a priority. However, from a Polish perspective it was a key sector and one for which Poland had an established export reputation. In 1991, the meat sector accounted for 2.5 per cent of Polish GDP (Cieslik, 1994).

In Poland, the industry consisted of about 1,800 firms. Of these, 64 were State-owned enterprises which dominated the market and accounted for 80-85 per cent of sales. Average sales for companies in this group of 64 amounted to US$32.4 million per year with some grossing US$190 million. Total employment amounted to some 80,000 people.

The sectoral study revealed many areas in which the organisation of the industry was different to that in many western countries. It also revealed a number of specific advantages. These included:

- The large domestic market for meat and meat products in Poland.

- The low cost of the basic raw material (livestock).

- The low cost of labour.

- The quality of the establishments; 26 held licences to export to the US and nine to the EU.

- A relatively strong financial position.

- Developed export markets.

Nevertheless, given the developing international competition faced by Polish producers it was still expected that some would go bankrupt. In addition, city-based slaughter houses were expected to be closed as environmental constraints were tightened and other reorganisation was required to face changing market demands. As with other sectors, the meat sector also held a high proportion of non-performing assets, such as hotels and apartments.

The strategy for such a sector as this was clearly likely to be 'bottom-up' rather than 'top-down'. In addition, outside the 65 large, State-owned companies, the majority of the 1,800 enterprises in the sector were already in private ownership. Individual enterprises were expected to take their own initiatives to achieve privatisation rather than wait on the white knight of a foreign investor. Some of these enterprises were, therefore, sold to local management and employees and the local community. Others, however, have been of interest to foreign investors. In this latter context, Poland somewhat accidentally fell into the 'green' bandwagon, in that most Polish livestock are still fed with natural feed.

The Griezno plant, for example, was sold to employees; the Opole plant was put into a Polish-Austrian joint venture; and the privatisation of the Sokoyow Meat Processing Plant consisted of a public share issue and a listing on the Warsaw Bourse. In another example, Polmeat of Brodnica, 60 per cent of shares were sold to local investors and the remaining 40 per cent to employees and farmers.

One troubled example is the Ostroyeka meat plant which was originally planned as a public share issue but ran up against opposition from the Solidarity trade union movement. Three other meat plants are likely to be part of the Polish mass privatisation programme.

Criticism of the sectoral approach has been raised in respect of the meat sector as not being one where significant international interest was likely to be shown *ab initio*. This, however, fundamentally misses the point that foreign investment was only one solution in this sector. Indeed, one of the usual reasons for foreign investment – new capital investment – was not necessarily a high priority since many enterprises already met international standards and a more domestic-orientated approach could legitimately be adopted.

The Czech voucher privatisation

The outline of the Czech voucher privatisation has been given earlier. It is worth, however, looking at how the early recognition of the need for sophisticated systems to allow the shares to be efficiently distributed and traded contributed to the success of the programme.

Two new entities were created as part of the privatisation. The first of these was the Registration Place Trading System (RMS) which dealt with the money transfers. The second was the Centre for Securities (SCP) responsible for depository services and a legal and supervisory structure.

The RMS was required to take account of the fact that reform of the banking sector had not kept pace with the needs of privatisation. Although a private sector enterprise, RMS was intended to provide a comprehensive framework of control which would allow individual citizens to place orders to buy and sell shares directly without having to go through intermediaries. As such the framework was designed to be suitable for an internationally recognised Stock Exchange.

The network on which the RMS was based consisted of many individual share shops throughout the country using sophisticated technology, such as networked computer systems, videotext and optical readers. Trade-matching could, therefore, be provided in order to ensure that cash and shares were matched before transfer occurred.

The SCP was required to link the share market organisations to a central depository without the need for paper/share certificates and with a settlement time of one to three days after trade-matching. This network was based on over 1,000 PCs in place across the country.

These two systems led to the rapid formation of a successful, secondary share market and the only successful paperless share transaction system in Europe at the time. The momentum created by this whole exercise which was truly vast helped carry the enthusiasm generated by the voucher privatisation through to reality for the new share-owners. Such systems not only, of course, benefit local share-owners but provide comfort to foreign capital interested in investing through the medium of the Stock Exchange.

As with the other case studies, with the exception of the Polish meat sector, the work was undertaken under funding from the British Know How Fund.

5

Rebuilding Local Industry

The restructuring of individual companies falls into two broad headings:

- Financial restructuring.
- Industrial restructuring.

The former implies that the industrial and operational base of the company is sound and that what is required is new money, reclassification of existing short-term debt into long-term debt, etc. The latter implies restructuring of the industrial processes, work practices, product lines, markets, organisational structures and management, etc.

As we have seen, the approach to restructuring has generally been set in the context of privatisation; the argument has usually been as to whether restructuring should occur before or after privatisation. Within this context, there are two groups of companies to consider – those to be privatised where continuing State involvement may be negligible and those residual companies remaining in the State sector.

In relation to the first group, most governments have left restructuring as a separate task for after privatisation, or have assumed that much of the burden of restructuring would be taken by foreign investors or the new domestic owners of the companies notwithstanding that this approach may not have maximised sales proceeds from privatisation.

In relation to the second group, unless a sectoral privatisation programme had been adopted it is not clear that any concrete plans existed at the time privatisation programmes were enacted as to what would happen to the residual State holdings in companies not suitable for privatisation and of no interest to domestic or foreign investors.

In the case of Poland, for example, there was, as we have seen, a belief that the sectoral approach would allow the government to include loss-making companies in the overall packages of companies on offer to foreign investors. As we shall see, however, the belief generally that foreign investors were going to take the major share of restructuring was unrealistic given the small numbers of investors large enough to have the resources capable of making an investment of this size.

Indeed, an EBRD working paper (EBRD 1993 (g)) on private investment in central and eastern Europe revealed that significant numbers of foreign investors were unwilling to take on the restructuring of an existing company, preferring to set up on their own. This reflects widespread belief in the difficulty of changing local work cultures and the size of the restructuring task.

Table 5.1 *Percentage of western investors In favour of restructuring an existing company*

Do you agree that it is better to restructure an existing company rather than to set up a new one?

Yes	No	Don't know	Not applicable
26.5%	29.4%	35.3%	8.8%

Source: *EBRD*

Second, the approach of packaging loss-making and profitable companies together over-estimated the attractiveness of the profitable companies and under-estimated the marginal nature of real competitive advantage obtainable even from a genuine central European 'star'.

Placing the burden of restructuring on new domestic investors ignored the fact that in themselves they were unlikely to be able to provide either new management, focus, technology, etc to achieve industrial restructuring or to be able to access new funds to achieve financial restructuring, although, as we shall see below, some companies have been successful in this respect.

Significant problems exist for both groups of companies. However, there are clearly serious problems with the residual, State-held companies because of the restricted political options available. Governments clearly have a dilemma. On the one hand, letting those companies fail and unemployment rise will be politically damaging. Yet, keeping the companies going when there is no market for the products or the companies are fundamentally unprofitable merely postpones action and, in the short term, continues to place demands on central government financial support through cheap loans or other subsidies with attendant macro-economic effects.

With the possible exception of the Czech Republic, this dilemma generally remains to be resolved. Attempts to resolve it have included case-by-case investments from the EBRD and IFC and also special restructuring funds set up using EBRD and EU funds, particularly in Slovakia and Hungary. In Russia, it is expected that the G7 funds will be used for similar purposes.

There are some special difficulties with such funds over, for example, the effective compensation for existing debt and equity holders in the companies as part of the financial restructuring which these schemes provide and their perceived levels of risk. There are also problems in having clear identifiable objectives for the restructuring funds themselves. The principal problem lies in the selection and supply of suitable candidates for such funds.

Since these funds generally provide mainly financial restructuring, the implication is that the companies targeted by them require no, or only minimal, industrial restructuring. Yet, if a company requires only minimal industrial restructuring it is more likely to be able either to obtain finance on its own merits or better still, make an attractive target for a potential foreign investor. The risk with such funds is that they are used by governments to shift the burden of supporting loss-making companies away from the government, without tackling the underlying problems of industry and taking the hard political decisions which are certain to be required.

WHAT IS THE BASIC UNDERLYING PROBLEM?

From the point of view of industrial restructuring the principal problems are usually:

- There is no market domestically for a product, the rationale for which was export to the former USSR.

- Traditional markets have collapsed faster than new markets can be developed.

- New markets are already mature in those products or are otherwise barred.

In this respect, many local companies have chosen to avoid the real issues of restructuring by resorting to middlemen to sell their product, often in barter arrangements. While this provides short-term productivity, it provides the company with no real feel of, or access to, new markets; long-term development is difficult to gauge. Second, the margins are not usually good.

Other companies have been happy to keep current production at full swing by acting as sweatshops for foreign companies which provide the materials and designs. Again, margins are small on this type of work. In addition, the wage competitiveness which allows this to continue is likely to be only short-term.

In addition, a company may be unable to tackle new markets because:

- The quality of management is poor and unfocused.

- The cost structure is wrong.

- There is no real potential for profitability within its current organisational structure.

- Quality, packaging and branding is inadequate.

- There is insufficient working capital to finance a turn-around.

- There is inadequate capital investment and out-of-date technology.

Fundamentally, a country may find that it has no competitive advantage in the products it currently produces because the reason it produces them is due solely to the logic of Stalinist-Brezhnevite central planning requirements rather than any wider business logic.

In this case, government policies designed to reinforce those industries simply because they are there are ultimately likely to be unsuccessful. A wider strategy of identifying second tier existing industries or new ones in which the country could gain competitive advantage is likely to be more fruitful as a sustainable economic base. This requires considerable political courage but could be effectively integrated with a range of other government economic policies, including cultivating exporting companies and industries and more targeted, inward investment programmes.

In this respect, although financing is an issue, the major long-term problem will continue to be the shortage of suitable management skills. This is a problem now given the large number of existing companies within any industry which need good management to survive. Ultimately, it may be the shortage of management in these companies and an increasing or undefined burden on central supervising Ministries which prompts swift action in collapsing remaining State companies into one or two concerns and in substantial pruning of employees. The issue of funding is important. In particular, given the level of inter-company indebtedness in many of these countries, it is pure illusion to assume that the quicker old debt is circulated between companies the healthier the economy. New money is required to break that cycle and prevent a catastrophic collapse if the merry-go-round comes to a halt.

Failure to address this problem is, however, perhaps one reason why Hungary's initial advances in reform were not followed through into more rapid economic growth and development. In contrast, the reason why there may be less of an unemployment overhang in the Czech Republic than first envisaged may be due to the managed way in which this process has begun there.

REFORMING SECTORS

Attempts to approach restructuring on a sectoral basis have, as we have seen, met with mixed results. At least in Poland, control of the process was in government hands and the results are more ascertainable. In the case of the Russian telecommunications sector no control has been exercised and effective ability to capitalise on private entrants to tackle the problems of the sector as a whole have undoubtedly been lost.

Russian telecommunications

At the break-up of the Soviet Union, the old national telecommunications network centred on Moscow became split between the newly-independent republics. The old system was, of course, infamous for its slowness and inefficiency and made little use of the satellite network used to facilitate military communications.

Faced with the inadequacy of the existing systems and frequent complaints from foreign investors, the Russian government undertook some measures to encourage infrastructure development in this sector. However, the commercial needs of the business environment have prompted spontaneous, private initiatives particularly in satellite communications.

The Russian Ministry of Telecommunications and Rostelecom has recently produced a plan for the up-grading of the local network. The cost of this plan is conservatively put at US$40 billion. Despite this, some foreign telecommunications companies have pointed to the inadequacies of the plan, particularly as to how it is going to prevent the increasing fragmentation of the telephone network, which currently makes substantial investment in the network fundamentally unattractive.

Some foreign companies have been brought in to undertake selective upgrading and at least one local company has been claiming success in attaching sophisticated equipment to existing lines. In reality, the success of such partial upgradings has been limited. There is, after all, a limit to what can be done with old and corroded equipment.

The private sector development which has emerged has been diverse. At least 600 licences have been issued. Most of these operations are based on sophisticated satellite or microwave technology designed to connect callers in Russia directly with the west, and vice versa. Some are also providing networks within Russia between selected points. All of these networks are expensive and usually beyond the financial reach of most ordinary Russians.

As a result, a two-tier telephone system is rapidly developing over a large part of the country over which the Russian telecommunications industry has little control. This has a number of disadvantages for the future. These are:

- There is no reinvestment of profits from the private sector into the State sector.

- Foreign telephone traffic is estimated to have earned US$3-400 million for the State system which is now at risk.

- The equipment being used by the private sector is diverse and largely incompatible both within the private sector and between the private and State sectors.

Spontaneous restructuring has, therefore, provided little benefit to the general public and has depleted the ability of the State sector to access investment funds which could provide effective restructuring and long-term support for a hard-currency generating sector.

What of the role of the financial institutions in all this? EBRD's funding, for example, of the telecommunication sector in central and eastern Europe has come in for criticism because it has funded private sector developments as well as public. This criticism has been aimed at three areas:

- Private investment was inevitable anyway and EBRD as a lender of last resort should, therefore, have not become involved.

- The private investors were monopoly suppliers in their own country and, therefore, unsuitable to be the standard bearers of freemarket enterprise.

- EBRD was merely funding a convenient finance short-cut to these markets for these companies rather than development of the sector *per se*.

In the case of Russia, this criticsm seems churlish given the failure of the State plan to produce progress. In addition, given the low level of overall investment in the region, EBRD's encouragement of private sector projects may be a significant factor in making reform happen now rather than many years later. Second, public funds are not going to be sufficient to develop the sector on their own. Thirdly, EBRD working with local government might be able to exercise some control over the integration of public and private sectors to ensure that the confusion seen in Russia does not recur.

Polish pulp and paper

By way of contrast, the Polish sectoral privatisation of the pulp and paper sector has produced an ordered restructuring of the sector as a whole.

The Polish pulp and paper sector was one of the sectoral privatisations undertaken by the Polish government in 1991 and is, arguably, one of the more successful examples. Part of this is based on specific action taken as a result of the privatisation study. Part is due to current natural advantages, such as the low cost of Polish pine wood pulp, some 70 per cent of Scandinavian prices (Ljunggren, 1994).

Despite a major decline in domestic paper consumption since 1989, the emphasis on a heavy export drive and cost reduction seems to have paid off and in 1992 the paper and pulp sector was one of the fastest growing at 13.5 per cent. Employment in the paper sector also rose, at a rate of 2.3 per cent in the last half of 1993 (PAP Business News - 29 November 1993) and its productivity increased some 3 per cent over the same period. Few of the 40 existing mills have yet ceased production altogether although many of the smaller mills have no long-term future. However, industrial restructuring within the band of medium-sized companies does appear to have left them more successfully placed to take advantage of increased domestic consumption at more competitive rates. A bottom-up strategy is likely to be appropriate to their full privatisation.

In the case of the large mills, the privatisation study clearly pointed to the benefits of seeking foreign investors. In preparation for this, some mills have undertaken quite significant capital investment including out of their own resources. Five of the largest mills have, therefore, been designated for partial or full trade sales. International Paper Co. of the US, for example, has acquired a majority investment in the Zaklady Celulozowo Papiernicze S.A. (Kwidzyn) mill with a US$228 million loan package organised through J P Morgan, EBRD and IFC (Reuters News Service, 4 February 1994) with political risk insurance provided by OPIC and MIGA. The funds will be used to finance expansion plans at the mill.

The benefits seen from a Polish perspective of this approach have been to achieve a gradual rationalisation of the industry based on a clear understanding of market need, competitive advantage and foreign investment in a controlled manner.

REFORMING COMPANIES

The case of Videoton

A good example of a successful, Hungarian, individual company reconstruction is the electronics company, Videoton. Videoton was one of the largest Hungarian companies, manufacturing a wide range of products from furniture to electronics. Its former size can be illustrated by three factors. It accounted for 4-5 per cent of Hungary's industrial production, it employed some 20,000 people, and it had the largest industrial centre in Hungary to the west of Budapest.

Its key attractions were that:

- Twenty per cent of its sales were already generated in foreign currency.

- It was very good at manufacturing.

- Its manufacturing processes had received capital investment.

Its disadvantages were that:

- Its organisation was cumbersome.

- It was profitable in only one out of five divisions.

- Its management had an unrealistic view of the business, wanting to prevent any break-up.

- Its markets had declined, especially in the former USSR.

- It had specifically been orientated towards Soviet defence markets.

Early attempts to restructure and privatise were not successful and as a result Videoton was placed into State liquidation with debts estimated at some US$115 million in 1991.

The new business of Videoton

By 1993, however, Videoton had made a profit of some HUF 150 billion. As the extract of key performance indicators below shows, substantial improvement had been made in Videoton's performance largely as a result of western management techniques and transparent divisional management controls. It still accounts for 1 per cent of Hungary's industrial turnover and is now being courted by major international companies such as IBM Germany to assemble their products.

Table 5.2 *Main performance indicators of Videoton (HUF billions)*

	1992	1993 [1]	1994 [2]
Group turnover	9.5	11.0	13.0
Profit	loss	0	0.15
Subscribed capital	8.0	8.0	8.0
Own capital	10.5	10.6	10.7
Short-term debtors	1.2	1.9	1.0
Short-term liabilities	1.0	1.5	0.6
Working capital borrowings	0.4	0.18	0.15
Employees	5,700	5,300	5,800

Key

[1] Projected figure

[2] Budgeted figure

Source: *Figyelo*

How has this success been achieved?

There are a number of factors which have contributed to the success of the new business of Videoton. In the first place, the new owners represented a successful consortium of a local Hungarian bank and, *inter alia*, the senior management of a highly-successful private Hungarian computer and telecommunications company, Miszertechnika, the senior management of which was released to take a full-time role in developing the new Videoton. The skills which they could bring both in management, and in sales and marketing were crucial. Second, an imaginative financing package was put together which included the fact that the new company was absolved by the State from the liabilities of its predecessor. Thirdly, an intensive, industrial restructuring took place whereby the 26 former operating subsidiaries were re-organised into 18 closely-controlled profit centres in just four core businesses. Fourthly, overheads were slashed not least by a combination of a reduced workforce and efficiency. Fifthly, new markets, including the former USSR, were identified and the company adopted a flexible approach of accessing them including by means of joint ventures.

While all of these factors have helped turn the Videoton business round, it is doubtful whether any of this could have been achieved without the willingness of skilled senior management experienced in the private sector, to devote considerable effort to the restructuring.

Tatra

A similar story can be seen in the restructuring of Tatra. Tatra produced trucks and luxury cars both for the domestic market and for export.

Tatra realised after its privatisation as part of the first wave of Czechoslovakia's voucher privatisation that its primary need was new management to help solve the twin problems of US$110 million of debt and a rapidly-reduced production level. Earlier attempts to secure alliances with foreign companies foundered and the company decided to import external management. Three senior US businessmen, Gerald Greenwald, David Shelby and Jack Rutherford who operated together, signed a two-year management contract which put them into the senior management roles in the company for a fixed fee and a possible equity interest at the end.

The US management undertook an industrial restructuring involving reducing manpower, instigating skills development programmes and internal management reporting lines. Just-in-time stock controls were introduced and new markets actively explored despite recession in the European truck market.

Financial restructuring has also been undertaken including converting short-term debt to medium-term debt and seeking new finance.

The level of success achieved in Tatra does not make such a successful story for Videoton. Losses were still made in 1993. However, the turnaround at Tatra is beginning with key decisions such as employment levels, business focus (should they stay in luxury cars?) now being addressed. The decision to bring in western management on short-term, incentive-related contracts was imaginative and, as in the case of Videoton, was crucial to the future success of the company despite subsequent public questioning of the move. Specific industrial restructuring undertaken so far includes putting production into one shift at most factories and cutting the complexity of products produced. Already a 5 per cent productivity improvement has been demonstrated and wider worldwide links are being sought. Financial restructuring is now occurring alongside the industrial restructuring.

Table 5.3 *Key performance indicators of Tatra*

	1993	*1994* [1]
Production of funds	2,950	4,500
Workforce	9,345	8,200
Losses	Kc 1.5 billion	N/A

Key

[1] = Budgeted figures

Source: *CTK Business News*

CONCLUSIONS

The success stories of company restructuring in central and eastern Europe clearly reinforce the message that a key determinant to success is accessing western management techniques and their successful adaptation and implementation. That this need not require a strategic foreign investor is shown specifically by the case studies of Videoton and Tatra, both of which showed commercial imagination in overcoming their difficulties. In both cases, however, the companies were privatised and were not part of the residual State holding. In both cases, access to finance and to financial restructuring could be based on a growing track-record for industrial restructuring, coupled, in the case of Videoton, with government assistance in the removal of the predecessor company's liabilities.

What can governments and international institutions do to help this process for other companies? The answer to this question needs to be looked at both from a sectoral point of view and from the point of view of individual companies. It also needs to distinguish between continuing State-owned companies and those substantially, or wholly, privately owned. For the latter, assistance is best provided by ensuring they have the best possible start (as with Videoton), with assistance with accessing domestic funds and by the provision of government incentives. For the latter group, the process needs to be substantially more linked to overall government economic and industrial policies than has so far been the case.

The second key determinant is the supply of companies suitable for restructuring. The selection criteria, if restructuring is not being undertaken in the private sector, should be rigorous.

In the first place, the selection of companies to be assisted needs to be based on the long-term assessment of in which sectors the country wishes to achieve international competitive advantage. Second, there probably needs to be a drastic collapsing of the number of companies in any sector in order to concentrate resources and effort. Thirdly, the government needs to have an industrial policy which provides incentives for these companies. These incentives need to be performance related or related to the achievement of other government goals, such as the generation of foreign currency. Fourthly, funding should be provided by a mixture of locally-sourced funds and international lending. But, finally, technical assistance funds should be obtained to buy in suitable management who are given a free hand to implement western management techniques. If a foreign investor is required, the government might like to consider specific targeting of individual foreign companies which would no doubt react positively to a package in which issues of market, management and funding were at least being addressed.

For such a programme to be allowed to work effectively more is required than a well-worded country-based business plan. Crucial issues relating to the efficiency of bankruptcy laws and the willingness to let them run their course need to be considered. In addition, there are clearly also issues relating to anti-monopoly trading and the regulatory environment in which such companies will operate. In this respect, significant progress does appear to be being made.

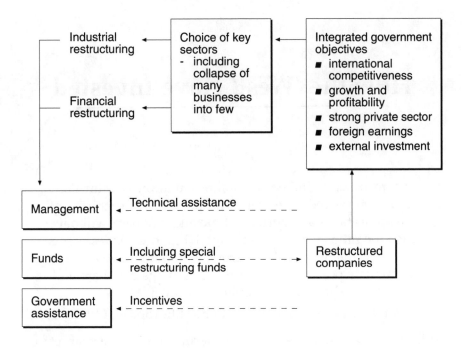

Figure 5.1 *A process for better restructuring*

6

How the 'West' Have Invested

There are only limited possibilities to improve return on capital employed [in eastern Europe]. The restructuring of companies takes an enormous time and pay-back will never reach the ratios we obtain through UK and US investments. Investment in central Europe would not have any immediate positive impact on our earnings per share and should, in my opinion, be avoided.

Alexander Notter, Hanson Plc (Central European, *October 1991*)

This somewhat negative and short-term view of the markets of central and eastern Europe is, judging by the amount of foreign investment made into the region, shared by many of the world's major companies.

By 1993 the amount of cumulative, committed (rather than made), direct foreign investment in the major central and east European countries had been US$71,090.7 million, split as shown in Table 6.1 below.

Table 6.1 *Cumulative foreign investments:*
1 January 1990 - 31 December 1993

	Foreign direct investment US$ Source: EEIM Cumulative total to 31 December 1993	Foreign direct investment US$ Source: UNECE Cumulative total to 31 December 1993	1993 population (million)	Main reforms began
Bulgaria	US$418.8 million	US$200 million	8.42	1987
Russia	US$11,587.3 million	US$3,153.2 million	148.77	1987
Czech Republic	US$11,697.4 million	US$2,053 million	10.3	1991
Hungary	US$9,268.8 million	US$6,005.7 million	10.29	1988
Poland	US$10,070.2 million	US$2,100 million	38.5	1989
Romania	US$795.1 million	US$755 million	23.0	1991
Slovakia	US$1,119.6 million	US$380 million	5.3	1991
Other	US$26,133.5 million	US$4,853.1 million	N/A	various

Source: *EEIM, EBRD, UNECE, Various*

These figures need to be interpreted with some care. The UN Economic Commission for Europe figures are based on actual registered investment. EEIM's figures are based on initial investment cost, eg acquisition price, plus future commitments until the project breaks even. It is, therefore, a useful indicator of future commitments and intentions. Even within UNECE's figures, however, there are wide differences between, and within, countries as to the methodology used to compile these figures.

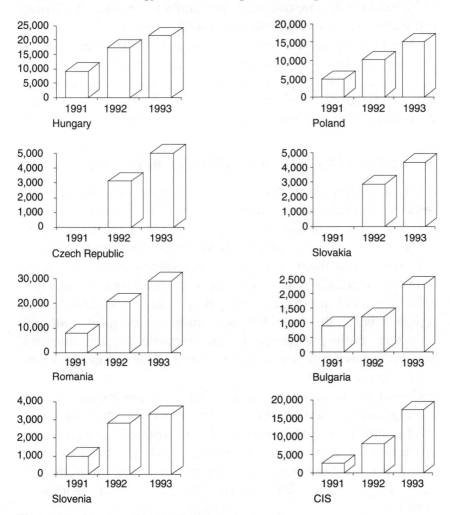

Figure 6.1 *Number of foreign investment enterprises*

Source: *United Nations Economic Commission for Europe*

What do these figures really tell us about foreign investment? To what extent do these figures represent a stream of small niche investments or one or two large investments? In Romania, for example, as at January 1994 the average size of foreign investment represented by the total foreign investment was actually only US$24,000 (*Central European*, March 1994). As numbers of investments have increased (see Figure 6.1), have average values declined?

In Russia, the share of foreign investment in Russia's industrial production at the end of 1993 was only 2.3 per cent.

Overall in central and eastern Europe as at 31 December 1993, 50 per cent of the total foreign investment by value had been committed by only 15 per cent of the companies investing there in only two sectors – oil and gas, and automotive. The average size of the remaining investments was only US$10 million.

HOW HAS THE INVESTMENT BEEN MADE?

Figure 6.2 below shows that, with the exception of Russia, in the principal central and east European countries there is an almost even distribution of the three major methods of investing – joint ventures, acquisitions and greenfield sites – but that the value of the investments made in each of these three categories is quite different. Acquisitions are, for example, particularly expensive and reflect the political difficulties of getting cheap deals. The Russian figures clearly illustrate the predominance of joint ventures, reflecting both preference in an unstable market and the possibilities available legally for foreign investment in the period to 31 December 1993.

One of the more recent changes has been the increase in low value greenfield sites. Until recently, greenfield sites had found favour with local governments only in areas of high structural unemployment. In other areas, they had not been seen as contributing to the privatisation process or to the diminution of State obligations by, for example, the purchase of redundant factories.

Poland

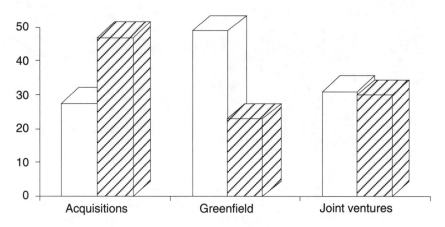

Key
ZZZ Value of deals
☐ Number of deals

Hungary

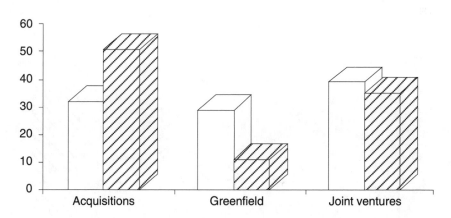

Key
ZZZ Value of deals
☐ Number of deals

Figure 6.2 *Methods of foreign investment*

Czech Republic

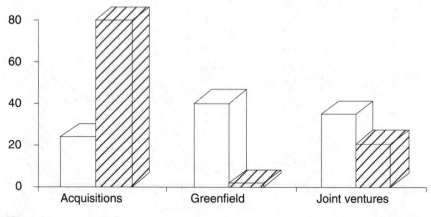

Russia

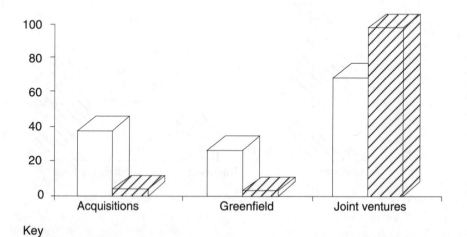

Figure 6.2 *Methods of foreign investment (continued)*

The increase in greenfield investments illustrates a recognition by foreign investors of two major factors:

- First, joint ventures are risky, rarely survive for any length of time and rarely provide mutual synergy (but are useful in less accessible countries such as Russia).

- Second, the cost of making an acquisition is significantly high.

It also takes into account a third factor which is entirely east European in origin and design. Whatever central governments may say in encouraging foreign investment, at the local level there is often still a mixture of resentment at the family silver being sold at perceived basement prices and the presence of definite protectionism (often leading to obstruction) where a project is competitive with existing local businesses. This also has to be seen in the context of the growth of powerful private trade associations in some areas which have effective blocking rights on foreign investment.

For example, in one recent study, a heavy engineering proposition was put to a number of regional administrations (*voivodships*) in southern Poland and to the principal trade association in the north-east of the Czech Republic. Whereas the former indicated wide welcome for the proposition, the latter were notably more suspicious in view of similar local businesses existing in the area even although most of them may have already been technically bankrupt.

The small greenfield operation, therefore, allows a foreign investor to dip below the threshold of recognition, keep his plans close to his chest and gradually build up a presence and trust in the local market on the basis of familiarity and good intent.

THE EXPECTATIONS' GAP

The need for such subterfuge suggests that there is a more deep-seated expectations' gap between what the locals want out of the foreign investment and what the foreign investor wants. These two may themselves be different from what the government is offering as vendor.

The history of foreign investment in central and eastern Europe has taken a predictable path. Initially, the emphasis was on non-threatening joint ventures where the foreign party had no more than 49 per cent of the venture and both sides could get to know each other. This ignored the fact that a foreign investor was unlikely to want to transfer much cash or technology into an experimental vehicle over which he had no control. Subsequently the foreign party was allowed up to 100 per cent and, finally, the foreign party could buy directly into a local company as it was privatised. Now, investment is being made directly into the private sector either through the local Stock Exchanges or into privately-owned companies themselves. In these cases there is less of a deep-seated expectations' gap between buyer and seller since both parties approach the transaction from a mutually commercial point of view. As the private sector grows it is likely that the expectations' gap will be reduced.

The speed with which the process of liberalising foreign investment moved was often dictated by political concerns. The underlying buy-in from the people was left lagging behind.

There is every reason to believe that when central and eastern Europe opened its doors, they expected a rush of foreign investment to come in and they expected that foreign investment to make a substantial contribution to the reform process itself and to fulfilling, in large measure, the capital requirements of local industry and the insatiable need for new technology and better management. There was little realistic appreciation of the levels of investment funds available, or that central and eastern Europe was but one emerging market in an increasingly globalised market place in which the competition for investment was intense.

Central and eastern Europe opened its doors just as Europe was about to descend into recession. By the time Europe began to come out of recession, world markets had changed and new and exciting emerging markets, such as China and Vietnam, seemed to offer equal, or better, opportunities and equal, or better, returns on investments.

There was also only partial realisation that the capital requirements could be effectively sourced only by the development of local industry and painstaking, local wealth creation.

WHAT ARE THE CAPITAL REQUIREMENTS OF CENTRAL AND EASTERN EUROPE?

Table 6.2 below shows a compilation made by EBRD of capital requirement estimates for the region. The amount of actual foreign investment is illustrated in the same table to show how small a percentage of capital requirement needs have been fulfilled by foreign investment. It also illustrates the unrealistic nature of the expectations, that foreign investment could in any way begin to satisfy such huge requirements on their own. Even here, of course, not all of the foreign investment is productive for local purposes, as varying percentages of the profit are expatriated to the home country of the investor and not reinvested.

Table 6.2 *Estimates of capital requirements in central and eastern Europe*

Source	Countries	Average annual investment needs (US$ billion)	Target years	Cumulative committed foreign investment to to 31 December 1993 (US$ billion)
1.	B, Cz, H, P, Ro	103-226	10	32.5
2.	B, Cz, H, P, Ro	110	10	32.5
3.	B, Cz, H, P, Ro, CIS	1,585	10	55.5
4.	Cz, H, P, CIS	813	10-15	55
5.	B, Cz, H, P, Ro, CIS	181-214 (gross)	1995-2000	57
6.	B, Cz, H, P, Ro	260 (gross)	10	32.5
7.	CIS	299-321 (gross)	1995	24

Key
1. Begg: target = 7% pa average GDP growth
2. Fitoussi and Phelps: target = average labour productivity = 1990 Germany and France
3. Collins and Rodrik: target = average labour productivity in the West
4. Gros and Steinherr: budget = average GDP growth rate
5. Ochel: target = 3-5% pa average GDP growth rate
6. Boote: target = productivity level
7. Korolev and Luschin: target = maintain production level
B = Bulgaria, Cz = former Czechoslovakia, H = Hungary, P = Poland, Ro = Romania, CIS = Commonwealth of Independent States.

Source: *EBRD, EEIM*

THE CONTRIBUTION INVESTORS CAN MAKE

What contribution can foreign investment make to the reform process? Can it support it, ruin it or even kick-start it? The response to this question is complex.

At one level, some commentators (eg PlanEcon) have pointed to the relatively favourable levels of foreign investment as a percentage of GDP which the central and east European countries enjoy, particularly when compared with other developing economies: some are currently around 5 per cent. However, such a comparison is potentially misleading for a number of reasons.

First, the percentage of foreign investment is, as Tables 6.1 and 6.2 and Figure 6.1 above suggest, over-influenced by a small number of large investments. The tendency with investments of this size is that they operate as self-contained islands within the local economy. Second, the comparison is only valid if there are no distorting features of the local economies. In the case of central and eastern Europe, some economies are still distorted either by the size of the residual State holdings in industry, or by the extent to which neither the State nor the banks are willing to use the powers of new bankruptcy laws to end the continuation of State subsidies by other means.

There is, therefore, no mystical point at which the foreign investment percentage of GDP suddenly becomes significant.

Perhaps a more critical indicator of benefit is when a single investment spawns a large number of small investments in related sectors, such as services or components, or seeks deliberately to purchase from local suppliers notwithstanding potentially greater risk. The simple effect of economic stability and job maintenance can be important, as the case study below of the automotive sector in central and eastern Europe shows.

NON-CAPITAL CONTRIBUTIONS

In addition to contributions to capital requirements, foreign investment can also bring potential benefits in technology transfer, management skills and export promotion as well as direct employment. Given the structure of foreign investment in central and eastern Europe – a few large transactions and many small – medium-sized niche investments – it is arguable:

1. whether the smaller investments can deliver these benefits; and

2. whether the rate of dissemination of the benefits across the rest of the economy is perceptible given the overall low level of investment achieved.

Perhaps the greatest benefit foreign investment can bring to a country is if there is a link between the foreign investment and the sectors of local industry in which the country is likely to be able to develop a competitive advantage. This raises interesting questions, which have been discussed in Chapter 5, on how such sectors should be chosen.

Foreign investors have chosen to invest principally in oil and gas and the automotive sector. Across other sectors there has been a reasonably even distribution of investment (see Table 6.3 below).

Table 6.3 *Principal sectors of foreign investment in central and eastern Europe as at 31 December 1993*

Sector	Number of investments	Value of investments (US$ millions)
		>US$ 10,000 million
Oil and Gas	283	21,801.9
Automotive	346	13,801.9
		US$ 5-10,000 million
Electronics	476	7,043.7
		US$ 1-5,000 million
Property	136	3,085
Engineering	221	2,863.6
Beverages	110	2,447.9
Chemicals	180	1,995.8
Mining	180	1,664.4
Tobacco	33	1,436.3
Pulp and paper	56	1,300.1
Consumer products	129	1,039.2

Source: *EEIM*

This fits in well with the general perception of the local, inward investment agencies which, with a few exceptions, have done little more than throw open their doors, provide a few, short-lived tax incentives and virtually asked to be raped. Few have identified what sectors the country needs to develop and then targeted and wooed specific western companies in these sectors for future investment. Such direct approaches would have been well received by corporate boards who would have seen them as evidence of greater commercial maturity and seriousness of purpose.

Given the levels of investment and the uncertainties surrounding its effectiveness in contributing to the reform process, it can be argued that, so far, foreign investment has made little significant impact on the local economies. For me, the best test at the end of the day is likely to be a cultural one of the extent to which foreign investment has changed the mentality of the government, managers, and workers to accept restructuring and redundancy, to liberate entrepreneurship and to lead to a burgeoning private sector of new small and medium-sized businesses, probably in the service sector. In this respect both Poland and the Czech Republic have made significant advances. The difficulty with this test is that it is difficult to tell the influence of foreign investment apart from indigenous progress and indigenous characteristics of entrepreneurial activity.

Some commentators have argued (eg EBRD, 1993 (j)) that the pioneers in investing in these countries can have a crucial effect on the attitude of government policy to foreign investment. To some extent that is true. The early reaction against joint ventures where foreign ownership was capped at 49 per cent undoubtedly helped speed the process to allow 100 per cent foreign-owned companies and even acquisitions.

On the other hand, with a few exceptions, the pioneers have often been an unrepresentative bunch of businesses. At one end of the scale have been small and medium-sized entrepreneurs operating on the margins where fiscal concessions may be crucial to profitability; at the other end of the scale have been major multinationals which in some cases have expected concessions of such magnitude that they effectively would allow them to operate outside the law applicable to other foreign investors. Both extremes may have helped deflect government policy into blind alleys and legislation much of which has since had to be repealed because it was inappropriate for the long term.

WHY A LACK OF INVESTMENT?

What are the reasons for the lack of significant foreign investment in all but oil and gas and the automotive sectors? To answer that question, we need to look at a number of separate issues.

The first of these relates to the motivation of companies entering these markets. In this respect, there are three groups. First, there are those companies looking to exploit the domestic markets of the countries concerned. Second, there are those companies looking to use a base in those countries as a low-cost location to export elsewhere. Finally, the third group consists of those companies aiming to do both.

This description explains what they are trying to do; it does not explain why. The list below summarises the main motivations for developing bases in central and eastern Europe:

- To take a long-term position as principal supplier on the local markets.

- To undercut rivals with lower cost products in highly competitive markets overseas.

- To improve efficiency and profitability in the home operations by importing low-cost goods or components into the home process.

- To secure access to limited, precious resources.

- To prevent competitors entering the market even if you have no intention of developing the market yourself.

COMPETITIVE ADVANTAGE

All of these motivations have one thing in common – the use of scarce resources to achieve competitive advantage. The question, therefore, is to what extent can central and eastern Europe offer competitive advantage?

In the case of natural resources, such as oil and gas, the answer to that question depends on the extent to which individual governments are prepared to sacrifice control over strategic resources for an acceptable return.

In the case of low-cost-base strategies, the answer lies in expectations that economic policy and individual aspirations will not bid up costs, especially wage costs, to uncompetitive rates. In this respect, Poland is most widely expected to keep its lower-cost base for longer amongst the three principal central European States.

In the case of all of the strategies, the answer to the question reflects the extent to which the local economies provide a stable base with long-term growth potential.

Above all, however, given that greenfield investments have been small in value and often somewhat tentative, the answer to the question lies in the supply of specific business opportunities with competitive rates of return. This has generally boiled down to either good joint venture prospects or, increasingly frequently, good acquisition opportunities produced by the progress of the privatisation process.

At this stage, analysing the extent of competitive advantage available is a complex matter. Clearly, some of the countries, while offering good acquisition candidates, do not have sufficient local market potential, may not have suitable locations, and may have too poorly developed an infrastructure to carry forward the advantage envisaged.

In addition, perceived competitive advantage may be eroded by the time taken to complete the deal due to government bureaucracy, legal process, cultural differences in contract negotiations, etc.

Realising advantage

While no one would reasonably deny that central and eastern Europe has significant opportunities which could confer competitive advantage, a number of factors need to be borne in mind when evaluating them.

The first factor relates to timing. In almost all cases the speed with which opportunities have become available has been linked to the speed with which privatisation has been introduced. This is clearly so in the direct sense that privatisation releases business onto the market for full or partial acquisition. It is also so in the indirect sense in that the management, even of remaining State-controlled enterprises, sense the competitive mood and are more likely to want to look at joint ventures, leasing, etc, if only to give management a potential bolthole as State subsidies are fully withdrawn. As all of these businesses are linked by indebtedness and formal trade relations, the domino effect of privatisation across industry is increasingly important.

The attitude of foreign investors to privatisation has already been dealt with in Chapter 4.

The second factor is the nature of the opportunities themselves. At the risk of over-simplification the opportunities have divided into numerous niche opportunities and fewer star opportunities. This point is amplified below. However, it is perhaps best illustrated by Table 6.4 below which shows that apart from oil and gas and the automotive sector all other sectors account for 85 per cent of foreign investment in the region as a whole, at an average investment of only US$10 million per investment.

Table 6.4 *Average size of investments in central and eastern Europe as at 31 December 1993*

Total number	%	Total Value (US$ million)	%	Average size (US$ million)
4,073	100	71,090.7	100	17
Oil and gas/automotive				
629	15	35,348.3	50	56
Other sectors				
3,444	85	35,742.4	50	10

Source: *EEIM*

Given that some of these investments, such as Procter and Gamble in Russia and ABB and Pilkington in Poland, have been major investments some over US$100 million, the average size of US$10 million overstates considerably the real value of the remaining investments.

The third factor, which is related, is that, as we have already seen, as a result of the specialisation enforced on the area by Stalin and Brezhnev, regions were allocated large monopoly suppliers for various products. It is these enterprises which are likely to provide the maximum international competitive advantage if their potential can be harnessed at an acceptable cost. But by their very nature, and their past affiliations, these enterprises are few in number, require significant restructuring, and are usually seen as national assets and, therefore, subject to highly competitive, international tendering at which the price is usually forced up. Turning these star opportunities into reality can, therefore, be a slow process.

One indication of this may be gleaned from the slow speed with which some of the major private western investment funds for the region were able to invest the money raised from western investors in local projects. Initially, opportunities were difficult to find.

THE PRINCIPAL INHIBITORS

One of the major inhibitors to increased foreign investment in the region has, therefore, been the supply of suitable opportunities. This has been a problem not only in relation to foreign investment, but also in relation to suitable candidates for the special restructuring funds which EBRD/EU have been trying to set up in a number of countries, and even for privatisation programmes themselves, as we have already seen.

A related reason for the low level of overall foreign investment may lie in the regional affiliations which foreign investment seems to take (World Bank, 1993) in relation to developing economies. Japanese companies favour Asia, US companies Latin America. Eastern Europe has to some extent been left to the EU with very little Japanese investment, and US investment directed substantially to the former USSR.

This has two potential implications. First western Europe has a geographical concentration of major multinational companies capable of making significant investment biased to the UK, France and The Netherlands, where they are invariably Stock Exchange-listed.

As the opening quotation from Hanson Plc suggests, major Stock Exchange-listed multinationals have, during the late 1980s and 1990s, tended to take a short-term view of investing based on demands for higher and more immediate yields per share by their shareholders and have not seen central and eastern Europe as attractive in those terms. In contrast, in Germany, Austria and Italy, for example, industry is more centred on medium-sized manufacturing companies which are family-owned. Without the pressure of shareholders and instant yield-demands, such companies have, by and large, been prepared to take a longer-term view of investing in central and eastern Europe, but have been more interested in the relatively less risky and less extensive niche opportunities, including greenfield sites, rather than the stars. Table 6.4 above has already shown the low average investment values to illustrate this.

The structure of west European industry may, therefore, have had a significant influence on the ability and willingness of EU companies to respond to central and eastern Europe in a more balanced way. However, as Table 6.5 below shows, the major investors by value as at 31 December 1993 were the principal west European economies with multinational companies and the US, an investment from one or two of which has a distorting effect because of their size. Austria's ranking, for example, would be significantly improved if the table had been based on the number of foreign investments being made rather than value, but is illustrative of the numerous small-value investments being made by central European countries.

Table 6.5 *Principal countries investing in central and eastern Europe as at 31 December 1993, by value*

Country	Value (US$ million)	Number of investments	Average size of investment
US	18,032	945	19
Germany	13,032	603	22
France	8,008	290	28
UK	7,437	288	26
Italy	7,378	189	39
Austria	2,572	440	6
Korea	1,836	57	32
Sweden	1,546	193	8
Belgium	1,313	38	35
Japan	1,300	141	9
Switzerland	1,224	160	8
Finland	1,029	116	9
Netherlands	909	118	8
Canada	570	62	9
Denmark	327	44	7

Source: *EEIM*

Second, the protectionist attitude adopted by the EU to imports into the EU of central and east European goods was not dreamt up by Brussels bureaucrats and politicians alone. It was driven by the attitude of companies in western Europe which were intensely hostile to, and suspicious of, new entrants to the market from central and eastern Europe. These companies were unlikely to be the first to embrace a central and east European rival even in a defensive mode and some have been pressing the EU to take anti-dumping actions against central and east European enterprises. The example of the aluminium industry is included in Chapter 8.

Unlike the EU with its initiative for the Single European Market of 1992 or the US and Canada with the free trade agreement, both of which appear to have stimulated an immediate increase in foreign investment, there was no comparable initiative with central and eastern Europe. The Association Agreements signed between the EU and the central European four on a bilateral basis reduced trade barriers over such a long period of time that they appear to have had no effect at all on foreign investment and are unlikely to before 2002 when the final trade barriers come down. Even the countries which signed the Visegrad Agreement (Poland, Czech Republic, Slovakia and Hungary) have not made a virtue out of the wider market potential the Agreement potentially confers.

THE EFFECT OF GOVERNMENT ASSISTANCE

Discussion of foreign investment into central and eastern Europe cannot be conducted without reference to the investment climate provided by the western governments involved and by the host governments. In various opinion polls (see Chapter 7) western companies have specified the following issues as major factors they are looking to see improved in central and eastern Europe before being confident of making an investment:

- A stable and predictable legislative framework.

- Macro- and micro-economic stability.

- A foreign exchange regime which allows profits and investment to be expatriated.

- The reduction of unnecessary bureaucracy.

- Improvements in infrastructure, especially telecommunications.

- Low tariff and non-tariff barriers and no export restrictions.

Fiscal advantages, such as tax breaks, do not appear to be a major factor promoting investment in central and eastern Europe any more than in developed markets. Rather, most investors seem to value more highly equal treatment with local businesses including employment, access to the market, etc. Frequent changes in government and in senior government staff have not helped to provide a picture of continuity and stability as far as government policy is concerned and will have further inhibited foreign investors.

Technical assistance for central and eastern Europe has to some extent provided support for the development of stable policies in some of these areas. Significant pressure has been exerted by companies and the multilateral institutions in this respect. However, this has often resulted in 'instant' legislation and fiscal measures to encourage foreign investment which have subsequently had to be repealed or changed as foreign investment policy has become more integrated with other government objectives. This has not created the impression of a stable, legislative environment.

The investment climate is also affected by the destination of the cash raised from the sale of a business as part of the privatisation process. The tension has been between the companies and investors wanting to keep the money raised from the sale of the business in the business to pay for future development, and the governments wanting the cash for the central exchequer in order to meet IMF targets, debt repayments, etc. This contradiction, more than fiscal incentives, has been a major bone of contention between foreign investors and governments.

More important in some respects, however, than the policies and incentives of the local government is the attitude and support of the foreign governments and of the financial communities in those countries. Advice, for example, from the Department of Trade and Industry in the UK that Russia was unlikely to be a suitable market for other than big companies with long-term vision and deep pockets is hardly a positive signal for companies to explore these markets, however justified and prudent the advice. Interestingly enough, however, small and medium-sized British companies appear to have voted with their feet and at least undertaken initial pre-investment feasibility studies, even in Russia, as the numbers of companies making use of the Know How Fund's Pre-Investment Feasibility Study Grant Scheme (PIFS) show.

The availability of export credit insurance is another key factor. Some countries, such as the UK, moved to privatise some aspects of export credit insurance (long-term cover), while making the remaining activities more commercially orientated with restricted government support. Domestic policies aimed at reducing public borrowing have deprived the government of a flexible and potentially successful instrument of foreign trade policy by placing too many commercial constraints on the operation of export credit insurance. Contrast this with Germany's export credit facility – Hermes – and it can be seen from the annual loss made since 1982, which reached DM 5.1 billion in 1993, that there are significant distortions in the western market.

Private finance from the banking sector has been weak across Europe but particularly so on the western seaboard of Europe especially in relation to debt financing. This gap is to some extent plugged by EBRD and IFC. The result has been that paradoxically there has been more equity finance available (including EBRD and the numerous country-orientated private mutual funds) than debt financing, although some of the equity financing has required short-term exit routes to be in place, diminishing some of its benefit. As a result some significant projects, including otherwise bankable hotel projects in city centre locations, have been frustrated through the absence of available debt financing.

THE IMPACT OF AID AND ASSISTANCE

To what extent have technical assistance and aid programmes assisted foreign investment? Leaving aside direct assistance through schemes such as the EC's JOPP (market studies) and the Know How Fund's PIFS and TIPS (feasibility studies and training), such assistance has overall been confined to general improvements in the infrastructure which, though vital for the development of the countries themselves, were not seen as other than indirectly helpful to foreign investors.

The attitude of the major funding agencies has been, by and large, that the private sector, and particularly multinationals, are there only to line their own pockets and should, therefore, be kept at arms' length. While this is beginning to change (Brittan, 1993), the amount of involvement of, and cross-fertilisation from, the private sector in assistance programmes has been purely tangential.

Comparison of assistance investment in the individual countries, even when distorted by largely incomparable statistics, shows generally less investment than assistance except in the former Czechoslovakia. This might suggest that there has been no real multiplier effect of aid on trade. However, it is probably too early to assess the extent of linkage between assistance and investment. Closer links may emerge in the future as assistance programmes move away from legislative and infrastructure support into individual company reconstructions.

Table 6.6 *Assistance and investment ratios*

	Assistance (a)	*Cumulative investment (b)*
Czech	ECU 5,082 million	US$11,697.4 million
Hungary	ECU 7,888 million	US$9,268.8 million
Poland	ECU 18,175 million	US$10,070.2 million
Slovakia	In Czech figure	US$1,119.6 million
Former Soviet Union	ECU 71,821 million	US$37,720.8 million

Key
(a) Figures are cumulative 1990-2 and include loans, eg from World Bank
(b) Figures are cumulative, committed 1990-3

Source: *EEIM, UNECE 1993*

Such assistance programmes also need to be judged in the context of the willingness of the donor countries to open up their own markets to exports from central and eastern Europe. As we shall see, the EU has bordered on the edge of hypocrisy by dispersing 1.6 billion ECU in assistance in 1994 to help transform the local economies, while still preserving a regime of tariff and non-tariff barriers to imports in the very areas in which central and eastern Europe has a competitive advantage. Admittedly, the process of dismantling these barriers has now been hastened. However, the EU underestimated the effect these barriers would have on investment plans.

After all, why should a company set up a plant in central and eastern Europe to export goods in a field in which central and eastern Europe has competitive advantage only to be told that these goods were 'sensitive' and, therefore, subject to barriers of entry into the markets for which the competitive advantage obtained from the investment was originally intended.

CLOSING THE EXPECTATIONS' GAP

Could the expectations' gap have been closed earlier? Undoubtedly it could. It is all too easy to blame western politicians for making excessive promises but being unwilling to support investors from their own country with substantial assistance afterwards. It is all too easy to indicate the distance between aid and trade policies; and, it is all too easy to point to the impoverished supply of real, bankable opportunities on the central and east European side. These are all macro-economic factors which may or may not have influenced the decision of companies to invest in significant measures, assuming a real business opportunity was there in the first place.

At the micro-level of the specific deal, much could have been done to reduce individual expectations' gaps and spread the word by changes in the style of negotiations.

Most western companies have approached central and eastern Europe from a basis of suspicion. Negotiations as such, dominated by lawyers, have inevitably been confrontational in nature centred on thrashing out the details of a legal contract which has only served to raise suspicion on the other side.

The feasibility study has been a one-sided affair, designed to get western Board approval for the deal in which the contribution from the east European side has been selective on an 'as-asked' basis and provided in a keyhole fashion without them being allowed to see the whole picture. Business plans similarly have been one-sided documents designed principally to demonstrate the return on the investment. Such business plans, which have had to be submitted with the offer document, have often been glib, vacuous promises of goodwill and unspecified future investment. That has been no way to overcome prejudices, explain differences and reconcile expectations.

Contrast that with the alternative approach. In the alternative approach the investment process starts from the position that the central document is going to be the feasibility study/business plan and that this is going to form a blueprint of how the venture should work almost on a day-to-day basis. It starts, therefore, with a joint high-level working party the functions of which are:

1. to decide on issues which will need to be thrashed out more intensely;

2. to allocate small teams made up of staff of both sides to deal with these issues and to set their objectives;

3. to keep an overall project management role on the process.

It is followed by workshops of the small teams set with clearly defined objectives and an outline of what they should be delivering. Such workshops are usually best run as intensive affairs located out of the office and away from home. They should engender a spirit of team-play and openness where ignorance about complex commercial concepts or about local customs can be raised in an atmosphere where no one is made to feel stupid.

The resulting feasibility study-cum-business plan becomes a joint document made up of the reports of the various workshops in which there is considerable pride and considerable commitment on both sides.

Outside advisers should be used selectively in this process but should include specialist workshop facilitation skills. Specialists should be available to come in and deliver advice as required but need to be attuned to the cultural complexities involved and be prepared to deliver some basic negotiating skills advice.

One aspect of this approach is that it is an effective risk management technique. Proving the reliability of the major commercial assumptions on which the venture is based usually inevitably becomes part of the task of one or more working party. In somewhere like Russia where the commercial risks are great, this may involve intensive fieldwork with local officials to test the practicality and reliability of those assumptions. If the venture depends on moving product from A to B three times a week using 50 tonne wagons, it is crucial to make sure this can be achieved in practice, and at what cost.

This type of approach is rarely adopted by Anglo-Saxon companies embedded in a tradition of legal negotiation. Within Europe it is much more usual amongst southern Europeans or amongst Scandinavians, where concepts of the handshake being more important than the contract, or of greater commercial openness respectively apply.

CASE STUDY

In order to illustrate the points made in this chapter, a detailed case study of the automotive sector in the Czech Republic and Poland is presented below. This illustrates a number of features. These include:

- the restricted and expensive nature of star opportunities (the car manufacturers);

- the wider niche opportunities available (the components sector);

- the extent to which one can influence the other;

- the ability of major investors to share the risk and extend their credibility by bringing in as co-investors their own worldwide suppliers;

- the costs of, and approaches to, major acquisitions;

- the interplay of trade barrier reductions and local incentives.

The automotive sector

One of the most dynamic sectors in central and eastern Europe has been the automotive sector. Of the cumulative total of committed foreign investment at 31 December 1993, the automotive sector accounted for some 20 per cent of total investment, made by just 8 per cent of investing companies. Despite growth in Hungary and significant long-term potential in Russia, the main focus of interest has been in the Czech Republic and Poland.

What made central Europe attractive to this sector? In the first place, in the context of an overall recession in the global passenger car market, central and eastern Europe, together with Asia (excluding Japan), were seen as areas of new growth via customer purchases.

One estimate (*Business International*) suggested that by 2010, central and eastern Europe would account for just under 9 per cent of global new sales equivalent to 6.6 million cars. However much these figures may now have to be downgraded in view of the poorer than expected economic performance of the central European countries, potential purchases are still expected to be significant.

Second, central Europe offered the potential of a low cost manufacturing base with significant fiscal incentives (in the case of Poland) if any investment was located in areas of high structural unemployment. In addition, there was confidence that productivity and quality could be raised to comparable standards to those in major passenger car manufacturers in the West.

Thirdly, the market was characterised by relatively few passenger car manufacturers – Skoda (Czech Republic), FSM, FSO (Poland) – which were separate from the non-passenger car manufacturers and the components manufacturers. Acquisition would provide sweeping access to markets. However, the companies were regarded as important national assets. An acquisition strategy was going to be competitive, highly political and would consist of tough bargaining. A cheap acquisition was unlikely to be realistic. Greenfield car manufacturing was unlikely to be a possible option in this context. All of the companies had experimented with some relationship with overseas companies in earlier years and were unlikely to be satisfied with a simple joint venture which brought no cash into the main business or provided a long-term, more stable future for the company as a whole.

Finally, the market has been in a state of change to take account of greater regulations, eg in more stringent emission controls and also in passenger expectation, eg performance and comfort.

The battle for Skoda

The most high profile battle was fought out in the Czech Republic over Skoda. When it was first put on the market, some 24 bidders from Europe, the US and Asia expressed an interest. In the end, it came down to Volkswagen or Renault. Carl Hahn, the Volkswagen CEO, deferred retirement to see the project through. Renault tried to bring political influence to bear by enlisting the support of President Mitterand.

At the beginning of the battle, most people's money would have been on Renault, for two reasons. First, Renault had an historic link with Skoda dating back to the 1960s and 1970s when Renault had helped modernise Skoda. Second, Volkswagen was a German company seeking to buy a Czech company located close to the Sudetenland.

Why then did Volkswagen win? Part of the answer is price. Volkswagen is reported to have offered 2.5 times more than Renault. But it also did two other things of almost equal importance. First, it made a big play of the pride Volkswagen would take in the Skoda name and Czech skills. Volkswagen promised that 'Skoda' would become one of its four worldwide trade names. Second, it made considerable efforts to get the work-force and management on its side by stressing the continuity of Czech input.

In contrast, contemporary press reports speak of Renault alienating the workforce to such an extent that they threatened to strike if the deal was closed with Renault.

The components sector

But the transaction was not a simple one of one car manufacturer buying another. At the time, estimates suggested that at least one-third of the Czech automotive components sector was in, or near, bankruptcy. Volkswagen and Skoda set out to secure their own supplier base and to spread the risk of the investment by a programme of matchmaking between western and Czech component manufacturers. By 1993 some 100 joint ventures in the automotive components sector had been signed or were being negotiated as a result, bringing stability and continued employment to a related sector.

How much this programme was an enlightened commercial decision and how much part of the terms of the deal will probably never fully be known but it has a number of lessons of more general application.

Subsequent results

Volkswagen's original price had envisaged up to DM 7 billion for an eventual 70 per cent interest in Skoda. That investment was to be spread over a number of years, although subsequently investment plans have been adjusted to recognise the European recession and Volkswagen's own position.

In the first year, the analysts who predicted disaster had their head. A loss of 50 million DM was declared. However, by the end of year two, profits were being made and production was up from some 170,000 vehicles to over 200,000. Volkswagen publicly praised the productivity and quality of their Czech operations.

Finally, in 1994 Skoda announced that it was also to set up operations in Poland, principally as a move to allow it to beat the high tariff barriers imposed by Poland on imports of cars.

Poland tells a similar story

Poland tells a similar story. Historically, Fiat had dominated the Polish market and had relationships with both of Poland's car manufacturers, FSO and FSM. Even in 1993 the Fiat-FSM alliance still accounted for some 30 per cent of the Polish domestic market.

In 1993, however, General Motors finally reached agreement on a serious investment in the market through the acquisition of 70 per cent of FSO for an initial US$75 million. This acquisition was far less public than Volkswagen's acquisition of Skoda. But, it had a number of features in common.

First, it was not a simple acquisition. GM are reported as being prepared to build a new factory for the assembly of the Opel. However, it is also going to develop FSO's production and help develop a successor to the Polonez. In addition, GM and FSO have, like Volkswagen and Skoda, entered into an extensive supplier development programme to try to encourage components suppliers to enter the market and bring stability to this investment and the sector as a whole.

What of the losers?

The main battles were for what were seen as the jewels in the automotive sector – the passenger car manufacturers. But the losers have not left the market altogether. Most have kept a toe in the market (and some much more than this) by moving truck manufacturing to Poland or the Czech Republic to take advantage of a cost-base which has been producing savings of 20 per cent or more. Others have established components manufacturing operations or have set up assembly plants using imported parts.

All in all, however, the battle for the central European automotive sector has shown the dynamic and active nature of the market in central Europe.

Remaining questions

While the details of these investments remain confidential, there are a number of questions which still need to be asked. First, to what extent did either government offer to prevent importers gaining access to the market if the investment went ahead? This certainly seems to have been a factor in Poland. If so, the effects of such overprotectionist measures are to be deplored. Second, to what extent was the need to bring in worldwide component suppliers part of the transaction or merely commercial prudence? And thirdly, why did the EU suddenly bring forward after the Volkswagen acquisition the date from which quota barriers for cars to the EU would be reduced?

The answer to these questions illustrates one point above all. The acquisition of a central and east European 'star' is a political event in which substantial senior management time and political capital needs to be invested.

PORTFOLIO INVESTMENT

Not all foreign investment is by way of direct foreign investment. An increasing amount of investment should be seen as portfolio investment either through closed-end mutual funds, often country specific, or through direct portfolio investment on emerging stock markets or through local bonds.

The former have been more numerous. However, central and east European funds are unlikely to be as prevalent in the future and central and east European opportunities are likely to be included within other generic funds such as European privatisation. Many of these funds have been based on optimistic assessments of the growth in GDP of the central and East European countries.

In relation to bond issues and emerging stock markets, central and eastern Europe has issued relatively few, internationally available bonds, but this is likely to increase as confidence in the countries themselves grow. Portfolio investment via the Stock Exchanges has increased. Two factors inhibit more rapid growth in this area. First, western institutional investors which might be expected to account for a substantial element of such portfolio investment are not significantly attuned to central and eastern Europe, still rate it as high risk and long-term and may be subject to prohibitive regulations in their own country from investing in markets which do not match their own regulatory criteria. Second, the markets themselves are relatively small, posing problems of liquidity with large movements in prices of often small blocks of shares. In addition, these exchanges need to convince investors that they have levels of regulation, reporting standards and investor protection which are acceptable to a foreign investor. Finally, there also needs to be improvement in the banking system to ensure rapid transfer of funds.

Nevertheless, some patterns are emerging which point to interesting possibilities. Taking the Czech Republic, Poland and Hungary, Figure 6.3 below shows the relative activity on, and capitalisation of, their Stock Exchanges.

The Czech Republic has high market value reflecting the input of companies onto the exchange from the voucher privatisation programme but has low turnover. Hungary, perhaps surprisingly to many investors, has both low value and low turnover. Poland, although with only moderate value, has a high level of turnover and a bottleneck of companies eager to get onto the market and take advantage of the bull conditions which have existed throughout 1993. In this respect, Poland's Stock Exchange turnover at the beginning of 1994 rivalled that of New York before finally crashing to more realistic levels in April 1994.

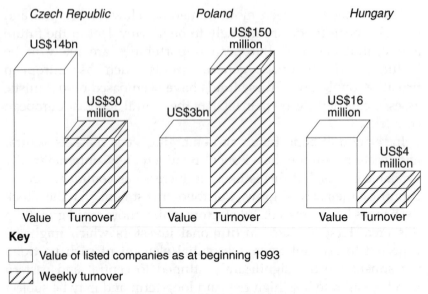

Key

☐ Value of listed companies as at beginning 1993

▨ Weekly turnover

Figure 6.3 *Stock Exchange values and weekly turnover*

CONCLUSIONS

This chapter has focused on foreign investment largely because of the importance given to foreign investment in individual government programmes as part of government economic policy.

Earlier in this chapter, it was suggested that the expectations of what benefits foreign investment could bring to the economy were significantly over-estimated. Rather than being one element of a comprehensive economic programme, foreign investment and privatisation came to be seen as the twin saviours of the economy. Neither on their own could make other than an uncoordinated contribution. Without supporting government policies for political stability and economic growth, expectations were always likely to be dashed.

There is, therefore, a suspicion that concentration on foreign investment has often been at the expense of developing more comprehensive foreign trade policies of which inward investment was but one part. Many individual municipalities, for example, are now beginning to put together business plans for export promotion rather than inward investment.

After all, what point is there in making 6.6 million cars per year if the local economy is not strong enough and individual purchasing power not robust enough to turn that stock into real orders. By the beginning of 1994, for example, there were indications from Hungary that the collapse of both export markets, hit by recession, and of domestic growth were leading to production solely to go into stock – a return to the bad old days of production-led policies. In contrast, the growth of car purchases in Poland in 1993 to some US$160 million of which half were EU imports shows the increase in purchasing power which it is possible to achieve.

Clearly, following the end of COMECON, the traditional markets of the former USSR virtually disappeared overnight with catastrophic declines in trade levels. As Table 6.7 below shows, the central European countries were successful in re-orientating towards the west and, despite trade barriers, to the EU. The large extent to which they were re-orientated to the EU, however, left them exposed to recession in the countries of the EU.

Table 6.7 *OECD exports from central Europe*

Poland		Hungary		Czech Republic	
Pre-recession (1992) exports to OECD		*Pre-recession (1992) exports to OECD*		*Pre-recession (1992) exports to OECD*	
EU	81.1%	EU	70.7%	EU	77.7%
EFTA	12.5%	EFTA	20.5%	EFTA	15.6%
US	3.3%	US	4.7%	US	2.6%

In this context, the restrictive policies of imports adopted by the EU became even more indefensible. The EU was an important market for central Europe as Table 6.7 above shows. For the EU to run a trade surplus with central Europe at this time was close to an international disgrace.

There is no doubt that the attitudes of foreign investors themselves have not helped. In my experience, that attitude has been based on an unusual degree of emotion and has been easily deflected by instant reaction to political problems, particularly in Russia. The perception of risk and instability has been far greater than the actual level involved.

In this respect, the 1993 Polish elections may be a turning point for foreign investors also. For many the unthinkable happened –

former communists were elected to government – and yet, the prosperity of Poland and the growth in its market institutions has remained largely unaffected and undimmed.

Central and eastern Europe need trade policies designed to increase the wealth of individuals and their ability to purchase more goods, many directly from the West. A key plank in this must be a policy of exports to open markets, assisted by decreasing imports through local manufacture and by general economic and political policies of stable growth.

Foreign investment has its part to play in this. But it is not an end in itself and should not deflect attention away from the broader trade issues on which future prosperity will be based.

7

Culture and Attitudes

The importance of culture and attitudes in the process of reform is one of the areas which politicians, bureaucrats and business people all feel hesitant about addressing. For many the absence of empirical data leaves an uncomfortable feeling that anecdotal evidence is selective and does little more than reconfirm established prejudices.

Yet an understanding of national culture and attitudes and of business culture are as much key determinants of the success of the reform programme as a carefully crafted privatisation programme. Indeed, the ultimate success of reform implies considerable changes of attitudes and culture, particularly business culture, which itself has implications for the nature and quantity of education and training and where these should be targeted.

Many companies understand this better than the international institutions supporting reform, particularly where they have had to adjust successfully to establishing a multinational, multiethnic network of subsidiaries. But in the context of central and eastern Europe, the absence of timely, accurate and relevant statistical data makes our judgements about investment decisions, for example, particularly prone to influence from our own cultural perceptions and our own perceptions of the central and east Europeans themselves. A poll of western investor confidence taken in Germany, for example, is likely to have a different ranking of countries than a similar poll in the UK, despite the statistical and market data being the same. This is most obvious probably in the attitude of the two countries towards Poland (see *Wall Street Journal Europe*, 8 July 1993).

The following tables illustrate the changing perception of the ranking of countries from a number of different sources. Taken over a long period between 1991 and 1993 they reflect clearly the differing progress in real reform in these countries and different ranking criteria. But how much are they also a reflection of underlying cultural progress in coming to terms with the new environments of democracy and a market economy and how much a reflection of the greater cultural comfort we feel with particular countries as our experience of them grows?

Table 7.1 *Changing attractiveness of countries*

1991 Ranking of western confidence	1993 Countries likely to receive future investment	1993 Competitive-ness	1994 Overall attractiveness for foreign investment	1994 Credit-worthiness
1. Hungary	1. Czech Republic	1. Poland	1. Poland	1. Czech Republic
2. Czechoslovakia	2. Hungary	2. Czecho-slovakia	2. Czech Republic	2. Hungary
3. Poland	3. Poland	3. Hungary	3. Hungary	3. Slovenia
4. USSR	4. Russia	4. Romania	4. Slovenia	4. Slovakia
5. Yugoslavia	5. Slovakia	5. Ukraine		5. Poland
6. Romania		6. Kazakhstan		6. Romania
7. Bulgaria		7. Belarus		7. Estonia
Source: *Central European*	**Source:** *MPG International*	**Source:** *World Economic Forum*	**Source:** *Ernst & Young*	**Source:** *Institutional Investor*

In this context, it is worth remembering that for most people in the West, central and eastern Europe has been an inaccessible and hostile region characterised by Cold War stereotypes. Most businesspeople looking at the area afresh are unaware of how rich and diverse the historical and ethnic cultures are, how educated is the population as a whole and how open to new influences many individuals are. There was genuine surprise, for example, that the level of productivity improvement in Skoda achieved after the Volkswagen investment should have been so noticeable.

These cultural perceptions go deeper than anecdotes. However, over the past few years there has been a growing number of more empirical studies which better quantify the cultural attitudes and better define the cultural perceptions of central and eastern Europe. Most of these are based on opinion polls.

Surveys of foreign investors have often asked them to list in order of importance the principal inhibitors to investment in central and eastern Europe. The principal categories have usually included infrastructure, the market and work attitudes and legislative stability.

An example of this is a recent survey in Poland conducted in June 1993 which showed the following as the main concerns (with percentages of people voting for them).

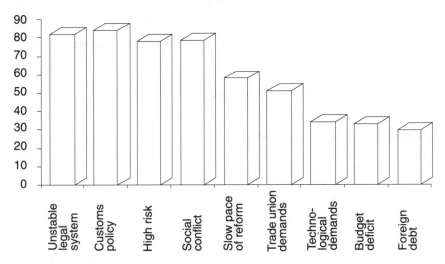

Figure 7.1 *Main concerns of foreign investment in Poland*

Source: *Rzeczpospolita, 9 September 1993*

In relation to infrastructure, the main comments have been about the absence of suitable physical infrastructure, such as telephones and roads, and the absence of financial infrastructure, such as banking and a stable legal system. Not surprisingly, these are also weaknesses which the central and east Europeans perceive as well.

In the following surveys undertaken by the World Economic Forum (1993), local attitudes to infrastructure problems can be seen to correlate closely with western investor concern. The exceptions are in the stronger perceptions of strength in infrastructure and local banking in the former Czechoslovakia. All figures from this source are based on World Economic Forum's usual weighting from 0-10.

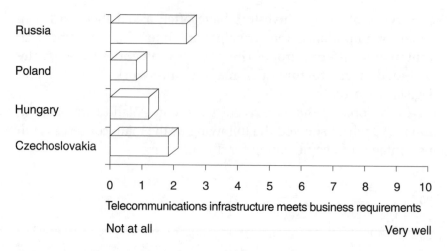

Russia
Poland
Hungary
Czechoslovakia
0 1 2 3 4 5 6 7 8 9 10
Telecommunications infrastructure meets business requirements
Not at all
Very well

Figure 7.2 *Telecommunications infrastructure*

Source: *IMD/World Economic Forum, 1993*

Russia
Poland
Hungary
Czechoslovakia
0 1 2 3 4 5 6 7 8 9 10
Infrastructure is a very serious hinder to effective business development
Infrastructure is adequate to support effective business operations

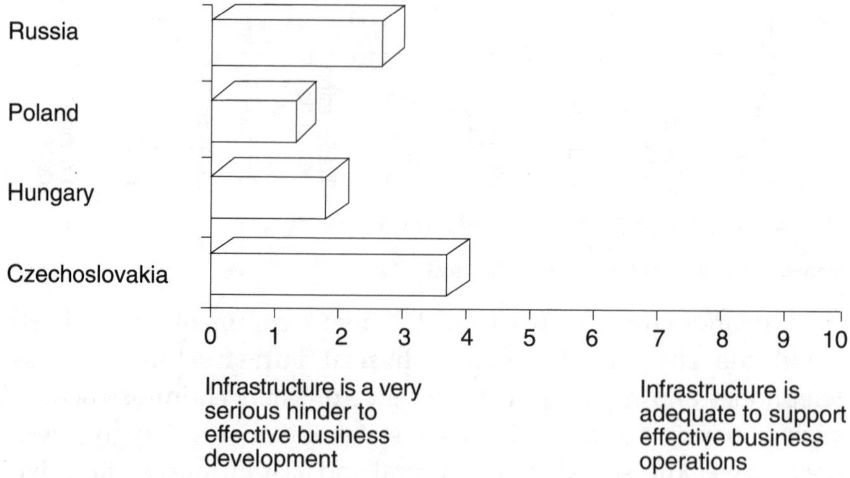

Figure 7.3 *General infrastructure*

Source: *IMD/World Economic Forum, 1993*

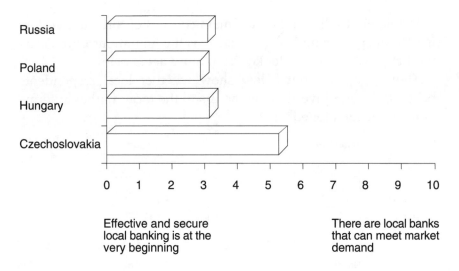

Figure 7.4 *Banking effectiveness*

Source: *IMD/World Economic Forum, 1993*

An additional factor consistently mentioned by foreign investors is the poor or continually changing legal infrastructure. In this respect, there is more divergence of opinion, with the Czechs and Poles more optimistic about the effectiveness of legal reform to support business activity than foreign investors seem to be.

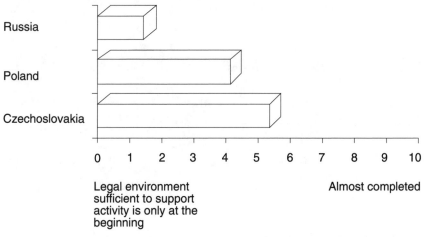

Figure 7.5 *Legal environment*

Source: *IMD/World Economic Forum, 1993*

In relation to the market, the main concern of foreign investors is with micro-economic factors, such as the limitations of the local market place. These are looked at in more detail below.

The surveys set out below show whether local respondents believed foreign investors had access to the local market in terms of the topic mentioned.

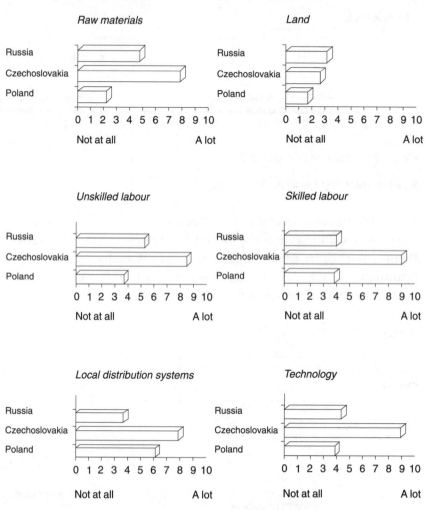

Figure 7.6 *Access to various inputs*

Source: *IMD/World Economic Forum, 1993*

Culture and Attitudes

While some of these polls show a close correlation between local attitudes to market access and foreign investor concerns, it is interesting to note the optimism of the respondents from the former Czechoslovakia. This is also mirrored perhaps by foreign investor confidence in the country, as demonstrated by the following poll of foreign investors which asked in 1993 which country they considered the most attractive for future investments and in which the Czech Republic lead the field (Figure 7.7 below).

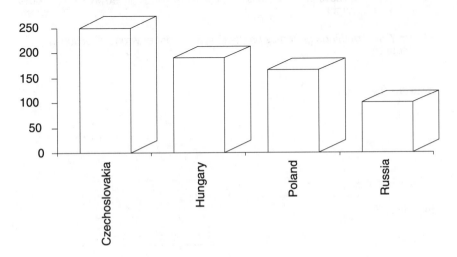

Figure 7.7 *Countries for future investment*

Source: *MPG International*

When it comes to worker attitudes and more general values of society, the picture is not so clear. One recent survey (Beresi, 1993) showed just how discontented the local population was with the progress to democracy and the direction of reform.

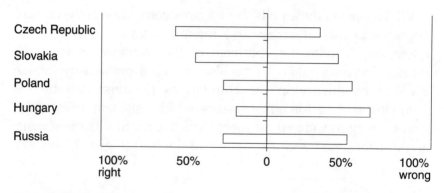

Figure 7.8 *Are things generally proceeding in a right or wrong direction in your country?*

Source: *Beresi, 1993*

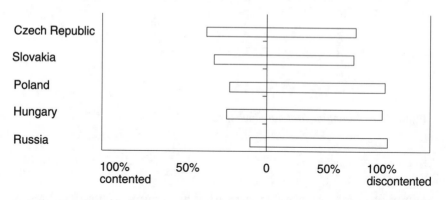

Figure 7.9 *How contented or discontented are you with the progress of democracy?*

Source: *Beresi, 1993*

These figures are somewhat surprising. The generally discontented figures across the region have, by and large, not been picked up by foreign investors in terms of political risk, especially in Hungary. The overall lack of optimism shown lies somewhat strangely with the clear objective progress to reform which has occurred measured by established, statistical data.

It does, however, perhaps illustrate how former-communist parties have been able to play on these concerns to re-gain political power and is further reinforced by Figure 7.10 below on quality of life.

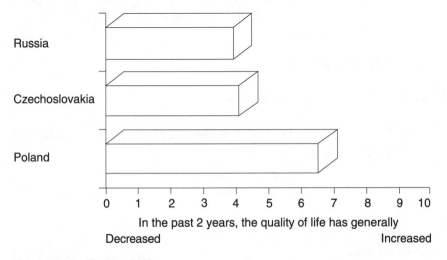

Figure 7.10 *Quality of Life*

Source: *IMD/World Economic Forum, 1993*

Attitudes specifically to work ethic also do not show the same high level of concern amongst local respondents as that usually admitted by most foreign investors.

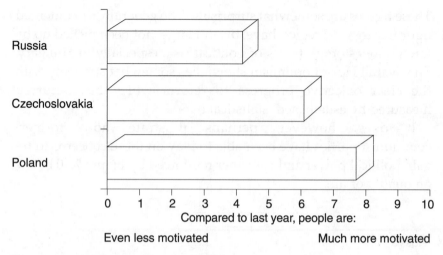

Figure 7.11 *Motivation*

Source: *IMD/World Economic Forum, 1993*

In the case of Poland the table shows significant belief in managerial competence.

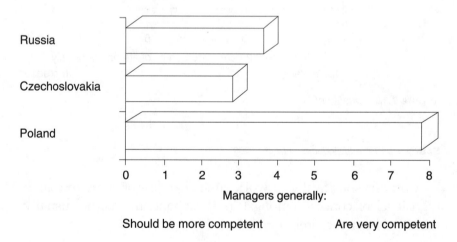

Figure 7.12 *Managerial competence*

Source: *IMD/World Economic Forum, 1993*

Culture and Attitudes

What do these surveys tell us? Leaving aside the different methodologies employed, surely what these tables show is just how superficial have been our perception of the attitudes and culture of these countries in terms of our perceived investment there and involvement in the reform process.

On what we and they both can see with our own eyes there is little divergence. There is, for example, a common perception of the need for infrastructure development. Beyond this, while the West has concentrated on the practicalities of macro-economic reform such as new legal structures, new financial systems, etc (ie those issues of concern to the West), it has largely overlooked the underlying lack of optimism in those reforms and the negative effects they have had on individual quality of life (ie those issues of concern in the region itself).

That this should be the case in respect of Russia is not surprising since it meets our expectations of the difficulties of transforming Russian society into a democratic, market economy. On the other hand, it is perhaps surprising in respect of more advanced countries and has implications for the need to integrate more closely economic, political and social reform in the way set out in Chapter 3.

In other words, foreign investors and economists in financial institutions have based their perception of progress and attractiveness on macro-economic factors such as GDP, inflation, unemployment, etc while the locals base their perceptions on micro-economic factors such as quality of life. The gap between the two is enormous because traditional economic indicators such as GDP do not include any measure of micro-economic factors or more importantly, of social effects. In a stable, western society with a high quality of life the governance of economic policy by macro-economic indicators is perhaps justifiable. In a fragmented emerging market such factors are at best misleading.

As a recent commentator has pointed out in relation to Poland (*The Economist*, 1994, April 16): 'Poles are materially better off under capitalism, but their sense of well-being has not improved in tandem'. A poll conducted in 1993 in Poland showed 48 per cent of Poles believed that economic transformation had let them become losers rather than winners.

Their determinants of economic gain or loss are not based on improvements in GDP and inflation but on continuing unemployment, State wage controls, uncertainty over future employment and an unfair and inadequate benefits system. This is notwithstanding the immediate but potentially short-term benefits provided by the black economy and the growth in consumerism it encourages.

The convergence of attitudes has, of course, been part of the pressure on the IMF to look beyond economic performance, to the wider implications of its policies and has been part of the wider questions raised by serious foreign investors as to social issues such as crime, union unrest, etc as part of more sophisticated risk analyses.

The exception to the general pattern of dissatisfaction is the Czech Republic where there was marginally more belief in the adequacy of local business infrastructure but significantly greater belief that the overall direction of reform was going in the right direction. As suggested earlier, this optimism is surely a reflection of the bought-in commitment obtained by the success of the mass privatisation programme.

CULTURAL IMPLICATIONS FOR BUSINESS

The implications for business and development projects in the region can be developed further by looking at the work of Fons Trompenaars (1993). Using a database of some 15,000 people worldwide, Trompenaars has set out to pose a number of consistent questions which are illustrative of a number of orientations of culture which he has identified.

These orientations are:

Universalist versus particularist The difference between societies governed by societal codes and those more influenced by special obligations such as friendship.

Individualist versus collectivist The difference between individuals as individuals or part of a group.

Neutral or emotional The difference between detachment and emotion.

Specific versus diffuse The difference between whole person involvement and the specific relationship of a contract.

Achievement versus ascription The difference between judgement on your record or judgement by birth, gender, age, etc.

Trompenaars also looks at two other areas: attitudes to time and attitudes to environment.

The purpose, then, of his work and the purpose of reproducing it now is to suggest ways in which culture impacts on specific organisations and how the effects of cultural differentiation may play a very important role in success.

As Trompenaars himself says:

> Nowhere do cultures differ so much as inside Europe.... The founder of the European Community, Jean Monnet, once declared: 'If I were again faced with the challenge to integrate Europe, I would probably start with culture. Culture is the context in which things happen; out of context, even legal matters lack significance.'
>
> *(1993, 8)*

While Trompenaars's work was not specifically concentrated on central and eastern Europe, managers from countries in the region were included in his database. Some general observations can, therefore, perhaps be drawn.

The first observation is that central and eastern Europe is not western Europe's or North America's backyard culturally. While 'western' management techniques are an essential component to the development of healthier economies there, the cultural differences need to be recognised. There is no 'one best way' in management techniques and the direct applicability of predominantly US management techniques is not likely to have a high correlation with success.

In addition, in contrast to the UK and the US, central and east European societies tend to be more integrated when it comes to business and personal considerations. Reform programmes, externally inspired, which deal only with macro-economic reform and which seek to achieve wider appreciations of the benefits of a market economy through changes in corporate law are unlikely to be successful. As the earlier discussion in this chapter suggested, the lack of reconciliation between the macro-economic and micro-economic can create serious underlying tensions. This once again reinforces the need for reform programmes to ensure depth and synchronity in economic, political and social areas and to try to achieve both specific, new-skills training and general education.

Indications of this can be seen from a number of the dilemmas posed by Trompenaars to his respondents. For example, asked to choose which of the following statements were considered usually true and for which most people in their country would opt, the central and east Europeans opted for seeing a company as a system rather than as a social group.

The dilemma was:

> A. A company is a system designed to perform functions and tasks in an efficient way. People are hired to perform these functions with the help of machines and other equipment. They are paid for the tasks they perform.
>
> B. A company is a group of people working together. They have social relations with other people and with the organisations. The functioning is dependent on these relations.

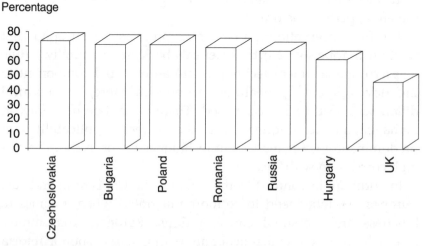

Figure 7.13 *Percentage opting for A rather than B*

Source: *"Riding the Waves of Culture"* Trompenaars, 1993

Culture and Attitudes

In these circumstances, the existence of a developed structure of corporate law and corporate vehicles (a frequent indicator of progress by foreign investors and development agencies) is no real indication of a change in other attitudes towards a market economy.

In addition, central and east European countries generally emerge as very particularist cultures (as opposed to universalist cultures, such as the UK and US). Whereas legal contracts and reform of the legal structure are important to universalists, they lose significance in particularist cultures unless a much larger process of understanding the advantages of the universalist preferences is undertaken.

Both at the level of individual foreign investor negotiations and of reform programmes, this point has frequently been missed.

The dilemma of Trompenaars which best illustrates this is the response to the following:

> You are riding in a car driven by a close friend. He hits a pedestrian. You know he was going at least 35 miles per hour in an area of the city where the maximum allowed speed is 20 miles per hour. There are no witnesses. His lawyer says that if you testify under oath that he was only driving 20 miles per hour it may save him from serious consequences. What right has your friend to expect you to protect him?

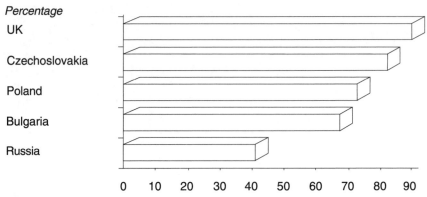

Figure 7.14 *Percentage opting for testifying against a friend*

Source: *"Riding the Waves of Culture"* Trompenaars, 1993

Similarly, other dilemmas used by Trompenaars reinforce the impression that central and east Europeans come typically from cultures with a respect for the totality of culture and where the interaction of business and personal aspects is high.

The implications of this for the world community are two-fold. First, there are significant implications for the way in which foreign investors approach negotiations with both local officials and company management. These include foresaking a reliance on thick, western-style legal contracts for more personal relationships, allowing more time for negotiations and ensuring that negotiating teams have sufficient grey hairs.

For reform programmes, the implications once again stress the need to approach reform on a holistic basis if real underlying commitment is going to be achieved. In addition, it is worth bearing in mind that the cultural perceptions of a cadre of academic economists, familiar with western economic approaches, who now happen to be in positions of political power is not the same as the cultural perceptions of the people as a whole, whose buy-in will make or break eventual economic, political and social success.

8

Conclusions

The bipolar world of the post-war years left us with a legacy of confrontation and stereotypes which concealed a level of cultural diversity long forgotten. When the bipolarity was shattered with the break-up of the Soviet Union there was a wide gap in expectations on both sides at almost every level, which to some extent was obscured by the emotional feelings we all experienced at the sight of the Berlin Wall coming down. Five years later and after many millions of dollars have been spent are we any nearer bridging these expectations' gaps? In the course of this book I have tried to show where those gaps exist and why, and to suggest what needs to be done at a micro-level to make the gaps smaller.

Economic reform has been the largest target of assistance and, not surprisingly, has been directed at solving economic problems. Political and social consequences and the immaturity of political and social institutions have largely been treated as secondary and have not received by any means as much international attention. Perhaps our sacred cow of the sanctity of national sovereignty has dissuaded us from treading in areas so clearly open to charges of interfering in the internal affairs of another country.

Economists are all too easy targets. But the higher the profile they have developed in the area, the more dogmatic they appear to have become in the rightness of their own belief and the more prone to self-deception as to the closeness of their theory and universally applicable law. For a generation educated in concepts of systems analysis and holistic approaches, the failure to stand back and see the big picture has been somewhat astonishing.

Politicians, too, make easy targets. Rampant self-interest has fuelled the competition between international and national funding agencies for the best projects, depriving eastern Europe of common co-ordination. Narrow self-interest appears to have prevented a common vision being developed of what the world wants to see happen in the area and, crudely, what it wants for its money. No common reaction to political problems, such as the break-up of Yugoslavia and the recognition of a plethora of new States has been possible. Someone, as in the case of Germany over Yugoslavia, was always prepared to go it alone.

Of course, this is the normal stuff of international politics. But did we not have in the end of the bipolar post-war world a unique opportunity to tackle a truly world problem on the basis of a common community of action? If we did, the signs of successfully doing so are woefully absent.

Initially, the largest expectations' gap was in the role we and the central and east Europeans believed that international institutions and the world community were going to play. Those expectations were excessive because the institutions themselves were facing a changed world for which their organisational structures, their philosophy, their skills and their shareholders were not prepared. Despite this, however, there were actions which could have been taken and which still could be taken to improve effectiveness and responsiveness.

IMPROVED CO-ORDINATION IS REQUIRED

The first of these actions would have been to have appointed one institution to take overall control of the process. That institution would have been responsible for an agreed plan of assistance with the central and east Europeans and with other international institutions. Given the small number of institutions involved, including bilateral funds, it would surely not have been impossible to provide a matrix of institutions and key areas for which they had primary responsibility. No doubt areas would have emerged where no institution had suitable skills. The idea of creating a new institution would then have been built on market needs rather than politics and would have had minimal overlap with existing institutions unlike the way in which EBRD was created.

Effective co-ordination on the ground in the countries themselves would have gone beyond the current G24 co-ordination to positive planning and direction, and ensuring common political conditionalities when it came to negotiating for loans, debt-forgiveness and technical assistance based on agreed measures of success and clear objectives.

Conclusion

That individual countries would have agreed to this, of course, has already been shown to be doubtful. As the relationship in Bosnia between the UN and Nato, and between the UN and the countries providing the peace-keeping forces show, world institutions were not set up to deal well with situations involving common aims and common control except in the specific political circumstances of the Cold War and the specific economic circumstances of 1930's-type problems.

This is not being over-negative, since the international community has provided some considerable assistance to central and eastern Europe. It is just that the method of delivering it and its consistency with other policies have been wide of the mark.

LESS PROTECTIONISM IS REQUIRED

Take for example the attitude of the EU to which I have alluded throughout the book. It can best be demonstrated by, on the one hand, its nobler instincts in making available 1.6 billion ECU in 1993 under the PHARE and TACIS programmes, while, on the other hand, showing the baser side of its members' nature in only latterly reducing protectionist policies against the import of central and east European goods into the EU.

To some extent, the EU had a point that in many key areas the central and east Europeans were operating still from a cost base which was not comparable with that within the EU, allowing prices to be kept artificially low: and yet, as study after study showed (EBRD, 1993 (a)) the effect on western industry even so would have been minimal, while the effect on central and eastern Europe would have been significant. All of this was often to protect bloated, heavily-subsidised West European corporate giants, which, in truth, were as much in need of privatisation and restructuring as the enterprises of central and eastern Europe. A rapid opening of borders and an end to protectionism needs to be embraced at both ends of Europe and beyond.

The case of aluminium

No better example of these attitudes can be seen than in the struggle over aluminium imports into the EU in 1993. In 1991, CIS aluminium smelters began a massive increase in exports which threatened to destabilise existing markets and which saw the price of aluminium drop to its lowest ever level in real terms. In a European context, aluminium imports from the CIS showed a dramatic increase:

Table 8.1 *Aluminium imports from the CIS into the EU*

1990	123,457 tonnes
1991	361,185 tonnes
1992	582,000 tonnes

Source: *Financial Times, 30 June 1993*

EU firms, particularly from France, lobbied the EC that protectionist measures should be taken to impose tariffs and quotas on aluminium imports from the CIS perceived as being threatening to existing jobs. The argument for quotas was based on assumptions that CIS costs were artificially low due to subsidised raw material, energy and transportation costs.

In fact, the EU consumed, in 1992, some 4.76 million tonnes of aluminium out of a domestic production of only some two million tonnes. The bulk of CIS exports went to Japan and the US. Furthermore, contemporary independent studies showed that CIS costs as a percentage of similar western costs significantly increased over the period as deregulation occurred within the CIS.

Table 8.2 *CIS aluminium production costs as a percentage of western costs*

1990	3%
1992	46%
mid 1993	61%
November 1993	94%
April 1994	100% +

Source: *Financial Times, 3 December 1993*

In addition, Intercomalum, the CIS producers' association did appear to be ready to make cuts in production.

Conclusion

In a unilateral action on 7 August 1993, the EC imposed tough quota restrictions on the importing of CIS aluminium into the EU, in which France was all but exempted from having to take any CIS imports. The futility of this attempt to control the free flow and price of a world commodity could be seen in the continuing fall of aluminium prices worldwide after the quotas were imposed rather than their increase.

This action also stood in marked contrast to the attitude expressed by Alcoa, the Aluminium Company of America, which announced a reduction in US production in 1993 of almost 25 per cent and job lay-offs of 750 (*Financial Times*, 30 June 1993) on the grounds of 'a lack of any mechanism to deal with the economic consequences of the dissolution of the former Soviet Union' and a belief that protectionist action from the US government would be inappropriate. This acceptance of the wider changes in world markets as a result of the break-up of the USSR is to be commended.

OTHER EXPECTATIONS' GAPS CAN BE NARROWED

The other expectations' gaps outlined in earlier chapters included the provision and effectiveness of technical assistance. Here expectations' gaps continue between providers of assistance and local governments and between providers of assistance and the private sector in their own countries. While the first expectations' gap has been due to faults on both sides, it is clear that everyone's expectations of progress in reform would have been better achieved if economic, political and social development had moved at a more synchronous pace. In the case of the latter expectations' gap, it is clear that a better relationship with consultants and a less stand-offish attitude to the private sector in general would significantly improve the scope, effectiveness and delivery of individual assignments.

In relation to privatisation, the expectations' gaps are more associated with the achievement of post-privatisation success of individual companies and the improvement in everyday quality of life. This is allied to the stability of companies and governments to undertake effective restructuring. In addition, major expectations' gaps existed between government and foreign investors as to the desirability of investment in their countries and the returns expected.

Many of these expectations' gaps come down to unrealistic expectations of sudden change and instant benefit fostered principally by local politicians, driven by emerging nationalistic sentiment rather than an accurate assessment of where their best chances of international competitive advantage lay.

Overall, therefore, are the expectations' gaps as wide today as they were five years ago? Or has there been a narrowing of aims and objectives? Is the West undeservedly smug and intensely myopic in its self-congratulation over having helped achieve what is predicted to be general economic growth in central Europe in 1994 measured by GDP?

NEW ECONOMIC INDICATORS ARE REQUIRED

The answer to these questions and specifically as to how wide the expectations' gaps still are is, of course, virtually the same question as whether our assistance to central and eastern Europe can yet be described a success. To answer that question we need to know the values of the questioners and what were the original objectives of both sides against which to measure the extent of successful achievement. That this activity is difficult to undertake is only partly a function of the absence of clear objectives at the beginning of, and during, the process. It is mostly a function of the inadequacy of traditional measurements which would be used to evaluate achievement and which determine the limited scope of objectives from the beginning.

Most institutions and companies have continued to look at progress in terms of GDP, GNP and other macro-economic criteria. As Chapter 7 suggested, the lack of resolution of the gap between macro-economic and micro-economic effects is a fundamental gap in the perception of change as a positive process in the countries themselves.

Criticism of the use of such macro-economic statistics has been part of the New Economics schools demonstrated by, for example, the work of UNDP (1991) and authors such as Hazel Henderson

(1993). They, and experiments in Japan, have forcefully argued that the established macro-economic indicators are imperfect anachronisms which say nothing about the integrated world in which economics sits. The essential point is that GNP and GDP are indicators of limited, money-related importance which are open to political manipulation and which say nothing about the arguably more important effects of economic performance which are based on perceptions of quality of life, human development and environmental costs. UNDP's Human Development Index (HDI) is one example of this. The new Systems of National Accounts being developed by the UN, IMF, World Bank, OECD and Eurostat are a partial tinkering with existing statistics which is likely to be an inadequate compromise (*The Economist*, 8 February 1994).

Yet, unless we can change perceptions of what defines economic success and how we can measure it, the dichotomy revealed by the development of central and eastern Europe will have been a barren experience which will leave parts of central and eastern Europe in internal conflict and tension for a long period of time.

Alan Greenspan, the chairman of the US Federal Reserve, is alleged to have received a colossal put-down from Vaclav Klaus, the Prime Minister of the Czech Republic, when the answer to his question of how GDP was measured in a post-communist economy was greeted by an expression of lack of interest on Klaus's part. However, this question, whether Greenspan knew it or not, was central to the debate of how well central and eastern Europe was developing and how best it could continue to be helped.

There is no clear answer as to what should replace GDP and GNP as economic indicators; but, if we are to draw closer together the current widening of the gap between macro-economic progress and micro-economic effect it is clear that it must better measure indices of quality of life and human and environmental performance. The larger the gap remains, the greater will be the generation of false expectations and with it political and social instability.

There is talk already, for example, that the countries of central Europe should be withdrawn from the major assistance programmes on the grounds that the transformation of the economies to market economies has substantially been achieved. To anyone, even in the Czech Republic, who looks beneath the surface and takes into account quality of life, human development and environmental concerns, such a view not only seems naive but heartless.

To achieve the flexibility required to look at macro-economics anew, international institutions could do no better than look to the private sector where investment decisions are frequently based, if they are based on anything at all, on a more comprehensive set of macro- and micro-economic indicators. Indeed, opinion polls of potential investor attitudes rarely stress macro-economic factors as a concern or as a basis in assessing a country. This recognises that a good business proposition can be made to work in a hostile economic environment if the business case is strong enough. In deciding the business case, the factors to be taken into account include a mixture of big picture issues such as competitive advantage, cross-border operations, etc, as well as the practical ways of doing business successfully in a micro-environment. A key issue in this respect is frequently worker expectations and the social obligations which the investor will need to acquire as part of the motivation of the workforce. Recognising the problems at the micro level, many companies have readily accepted, for example, that they will need to maintain unrealistically high levels of employment in the short-term in the face of the logic of the business case and market forces. Such decisions are based on perceptions of real change at grass-roots level as much as allegedly objective statistics.

THE POSITIVE ASPECTS

In outlining the negative side of what has happened in central and eastern Europe, we should not lose sight of the substantial achievements which have been made in what is only a short period of time. Democracy is now well established in many countries where communist dictatorships once reigned. There is a wider freedom of information and of expression including the press. Human rights records are significantly better and ownership of property is once more allowed. On the economic side, significant

Conclusion

amounts of industrial production are now generated from the private sector within an established business framework. Mass privatisation programmes have been successful in expanding awareness of and participation in reform and in transforming the nature of society without the need for a significant cash effect. Wider consumer choices are now available as can be demonstrated by the increased presence of key consumer goods.

Table 8.3 *Ownership of goods per 100 households*

	1985	1990	1992
Cars	27.2	33.2	41.4
Colour TVs	23.1	67.1	91.4
Video players	N.A.	20.1	53.4
Washing machines	38.7	63.5	69.7

Source: *Central statistical office of Poland*

In addition, with the exception of Russia, there is a generally higher level of national self-confidence.

The problems the central and east Europeans face, however, are in many cases problems of structural readjustment which are not unique to them alone. Unemployment as a result of productivity increases, for example, is hardly an east European phenomenon. Yet when it comes to wider choices of life-style and choices over healthcare and education, the picture not only shows less improvement; in many areas, it shows a decline. The expression of one Hungarian that they were freer but poorer is typical.

Reform in central and eastern Europe has, therefore, been a top-down phenomenon rather than a bottom-up phenomenon. The secret of success now would seem best to lie in the speed with which the top and bottom become part of one whole. Two factors above all are likely to influence this. First, real improvements need to be made to individual quality of life as soon as possible. Second, the West needs to realise that the process will take longer than they imagine and they cannot simply walk away when growth in GDP is evident. There is still much work to be done.

Bibliography

Attali, J (1991)   Address at the inaugural session of the Board of Governors of EBRD, EBRD, London

Attali, J (1994)   *Europe(s)*, Fayard, Paris

Beresi, J (1993)   'Hungary: residents feel discontented - but they're staying just the same' in *The Hungarian Observer*, April 1993, pp. 11-13

Brittan, L (1993)   Ep Rex Committee Hearing on Phare and Tacis 9 June 1993

Business Central Europe   A monthly journal published by *The Economist*

Business International (1991)   *Tapping Aid to Eastern Europe: strategies for success*, The Economist Group, London

CBI (1992)   *Economic Aid to Eastern Europe: a practical approach to the commercial opportunities*, Insight International Publishing, London

Central European (Various)   *Central European: Finance and Business in Central and Eastern Europe*. Monthly periodical, April 1991, Euromoney, London

Cieslik, J (1994)   'The Polish meat-processing industry' in *Encyclopaedia of Polish Industry*, 1994, 194-196

Daiwa (1993)

Eastern Europe and the CIS: economic trends and prospects, Daiwa Institute of Research Europe Limited, June 1993

Dewatri pont M&Roland G (1994)

'East Europe: Less haste more speed' in *European Economic Perspectives*, February 1994, 1-2 Centre for Economic Policy Research, London

EBRD (1991(a))

Operational challenges and priorities: initial orientations, EBRD, London, April 1991

EBRD (1991(b))

Annual Report 1991, London

EBRD (1992)

Annual Report 1992, London

EBRD (1993(a))

'Needed mechanisms of corporate governance and finance in eastern Europe' by E S Phelps, Ronan Frydman, Andrej Rapaczynskei and Andrei Shleifer, EBRD Working Paper No. 1, March 1993, London

EBRD (1993(b))

'Restructuring the Czech economy' by Joshua Charap and Alena Zemplinerova, EBRD Working Paper No. 2, March 1993, London

EBRD (1993(c))

'The threat of managed trade to transforming economies' by Sylvia Ostry, EBRD Working Paper No. 3, March 1993, London

EBRD (1993(d))

'Helping transition through trade? EC and US policy towards exports from eastern and central Europe', Brian Hindley, EBRD Working Paper No. 4, March 1993, London

EBRD (1993(e))   'A survey of private manufacturers in St Petersburg' by Leila Webster and Joshua Charap, EBRD Working Paper No. 5, July 1993, London

EBRD (1993(f))   'On the speed of transition in central Europe' by Philippe Aghion and Olivier Jean Blanchard, EBRD Working Paper No. 6, July 1993, London

EBRD (1993(g))   'Private Investment in central and eastern Europe: survey results' by Pietro Genco, Siria Taurelli, Claudio Viezzoli, EBRD Working Paper No. 7, July 1993, London

EBRD (1993(h))   'Heterodox stabilisation in eastern Europe' by Jan Winiecki, EBRD Working Paper No. 8, July 1993, London

EBRD (1993(i))   'Current Economic Issues', *EBRD Economic Review*, July 1993, London

EBRD (1993(j))   'Annual Economic Outlook', *EBRD Economic Review,* September 1993, London

EBRD (1993(k))   'EC imports from eastern Europe: iron and steel' by Zhen Kun Wang and L Alan Winters, EBRD Working Paper No. 9, October 1993

EBRD (1993(l))   'Domestic and trade policy for central and eastern European agriculture' by Larry Karp and Spiro Stefanou, EBRD Working Paper No. 10, October 1993, London

EBRD (1993(m))

'Common fallacies in the debate on the economic transition in central and eastern Europe' by Leszek Balcerowizs, EBRD Working Paper No. 11, October 1993, London

EBRD (1993(n))

'The behaviour of state firms in eastern Europe: pre-privatisation' by Philippe Aghion, Olivier Jean Blanchard and Robin Burgess, EBRD Working Paper No. 12, October 1993, London

EBRD (1993(o))

Annual Report, 1993, London

EIU (Various)

Country Reports, The Economist Intelligence Unit, London

FT/FEE (Various)

Finance East Europe, twice monthly news of investment, finance and banking in the emerging markets of central and eastern Europe and the former Soviet Union, *Financial Times*, London

Henderson, H (1993)

'Paradigms in Progress: life beyond economics', Adamantine Press, London

Howell, J M (1990)

'Accountancy in Eastern Europe' in the *Treasurer*, June, 1990, 29-30

Howell, J M (1991 (a))

'Planning for Central and Eastern Europe and the USSR' in *Hambro Company Guide*, February 1991, 44-47

Howell, J M (1991 (b))

'HungarHotels: a case study in the great valuation debate' in *Central European*, April 1991, 22-23

Howell, J M (1991 (c))   'Eastern Europe: an overview of the business context' in the *Tax Journal*, 30 May 1991, 14-17

Howell, J M (1992 (a))   'The value of eastern Europe' in *Hambro Company Guide*, May 1992, 46-49

Howell, J M (1992 (b))   'Investment in central and eastern Europe: What do companies really think?' in *Hambro Company Guide*, August 1992, 22 - 25

Howell, J M (1992 (c))   'Investing in Poland' in *Hambro Company Guide*, November 1992, 23-26

Howell, J M (1992 (d))   *'Planning for central & eastern Europe & the former USSR'* , Ernst & Young, London

Howell, J M (1993)   'Assessing Market Potential' in *CBI European Business Handbook* edited by Adam Jolly & Jonathan Reuvid, 1993, 342-347

Howell, J M (1994 (a))   'Development funding and private sector in CEE' in *World Infrastructure*, 1994, pp. 72-74, London

Howell, J M (1994 (b))   'The glistening bank: a review of Jacques Attali, *Europe(s)*' in *The Times Literary Supplement*, 4 March 1994

Kaser, M (1993)   'The marketization of eastern Europe' in *The New Europe: politics, government and economy since 1945* ed. J Story Blackwell, Oxford

Ljunggren, A (1994)   'The pulp and paper industry' in *Encyclopaedia of Polish industry*, 1994, 113-116

Bibliography

Milward, A S (1987)

The Reconstruction of Western Europe 1945-51, Methuen & Co, London

Morrissey, W O (1993)

'The Mixing of Aid and Trade Policies', *The World Economy*, January 1993, Volume 16, Number 1, pp. 60-84

PHARE (1992)

Assistance for economic restructuring in the countries of Central and Eastern Europe: an operational guide, Commission of the European Communities, Brussels

PlanEcon (Various)

Business Report, bi-weekly newsletter on Eastern Europe and the Former Soviet Republics, Washington

Story, J (Ed) (1993)

The New Europe: politics, government and economy since 1945, Blackwell, Oxford

Trompenaars, F (1993)

Riding the Waves of Culture: Understanding cultural diversity in business, Nicholas Brealey Publishing

UNDP (1991)

Human Development Report, New York

UNECE (1993)

Economic Survey of Europe in 1992 - 1993, New York, 1993

UNECE (Various)

East-West Investment News, United Nations Economic Commission for Europe, 1993, Geneva

World Bank (1993)

Global Economic Prospects and the Developing Countries, World Bank, Washington, D. C.

World Economic Forum (1993)

Emerging Market Economies Report, The World Competitiveness Series, IMD World Economic Forum, Geneva

Wrangham, C (1993)

'The European Bank for Reconstruction and Development' in *Project Finance 1992/93* ed. Stephen Syrett and Harold Fairfull, Euromoney, London

Index

ABB 119
accountancy 57
acquisitions 108-11, 118
advisers, outside 127
Africa 70
Albania, ranking 44-5
Alcoa (Aluminium Company of America) 157
Aliyev, President of Azerbaijan 50
aluminium industry 122, 155-7
anti-dumping 122
anti-monopoly trading 104
Armenia 50, 53
  ranking 52
Asia 120, 129
assistance and investment ratios 125 (Table 6.6)
Association Agreements with central European four, EU 122
Attali, Jacques 9, 10, 56, 59, 68
attitudes
  and culture 137-52
  of funding agencies 125
  of governments to foreign investment 116, 123-4
  to time and the environment 149
attractiveness, changing of countries 138 (Table 7.1)
auctions, public 77, 79
Austria 22, 120, 121
automotive sector
  Czech Republic 128-9
  Poland 131-2
aviation 5
Azerbaijan 31
  ranking 50-1

banking reform 66
banking scam, Romania 76

banking systems 133
  and debt financing 124
  effectiveness 141 (Figure 7.4)
bankruptcy laws 68, 83, 104, 114
Beck, Tamas 81-2
Belarus
  currency union with Russia 37
  foreign investment in 36 (Figure 2.3)
  ranking 36-7
Beresi, J 143
Berlin Wall
  fall of xvi, 1-3, 153
  consequences of 3-5
black economy 148
bond issues 133
Bosnia 155
Brau und Brunnen, Germany 88
Bretton Woods agreement (1944) 7
Brezhnev, Leonid 95, 119
Britain see UK
British Invisibles' Central and East European panel 63
British Know How Fund see UK Know How Fund
Brittan, Sir Leon 60, 61-2, 125
Bulgaria 67
  ranking 27-8
bureaucracy 70, 118, 123
Bush, George 7, 59, 70
business, cultural implications for 148-52
business culture 137
business infrastructure 13
business opportunities 13
business plans 126-7

Canada, free trade agreement with US 122
capital markets, development of 67-8
capital requirements

of central and eastern Europe 113
  estimates 113 (Table 6.2)
capitalism 76, 147
  world market 4, 7
central and eastern Europe
  capital requirements of 113
    (Table 6.2)
  foreign investment 106-36
  privatisation programmes 71-91
  technical assistance for 55-70
Central European Free Trade
  Agreement 5
central European states
  admission to EU 3
  possible withdrawal from technical
    assistance 159-60
central planning 95
Centre for Securities, Czech Republic
  90-1
centres of excellence 62, 72
Chernobyl 36
China 70, 112
Cieslik, J 88
CIS 6
  aluminium industry 155-7 (Table
    8.2)
  technical assistance for 55-70
civil service 66, 67
co-ordination 59-60, 68, 70
  requirement for 154-5
CoCOM committee 3
Cold War 1, 138
COMECON 3, 4-5, 135
command economy 3, 11
communism 1, 7, 58
communists, former 58, 59, 136, 145
companies, packaging loss-making
  and profitable together 93
company
  as a social group 150 (Figure 7.13)
  as a system 150 (Figure 7.13)
company restructuring 67, 92-105
  conclusions 103-5
  model of process 104-5 (Figure 5.1)
competitive advantage
  foreign investment 117-20
  international 4
consultancy tourism 62-3 (Figure 3.1)
consultants 157

individual 60
  naive use of 61-3, 70
consumer choices 161 (Table 8.3)
consumerism 148
corporate law 151
cost structure of companies 95
countries
  changing attractiveness of 137-8
    (Table 7.1)
  investing in central and eastern
    Europe 121 (Table 6.5)
country ratings 13 (Table 2.1)
credit rating, of various countries 13
crime, in Russia 32, 33
Crimea 48
Croatia, ranking 41
cultural differences 116, 118, 127, 148-
  52, 153
culture
  and attitudes 137-52
  orientations of 148-9
cultures
  complex web of 10-11
  continuity of indigenous 2
Czech Republic 5, 12, 34, 68, 96, 116,
  122, 160
  automotive sector 128-31
  foreign direct investment in 17-18
    (Figures 2.2 and 2a)
  infrastructure 139-43
  mass privatisation 74, 78-9, 148
  methods of foreign investment 109
    (Figure 6.2)
  OECD exports 135 (Table 6.7)
  percentage of GDP generated from
    the private sector 85-6 (Table 4.3)
  political/economic bridge 58
  post-privatisation 83-4
  privatisation methods 74, 75
    (Table 4.2)
  ranking 17-19
  Stock Exchange 84, 133, 134
  voucher privatisation 58, 74, 102
    case study 90-1
Czechoslovakia 5
  Velvet revolution xvi

debt-forgiveness 154
democracy 143, 144 (Figure 7.9), 160-1

Index

Dnestr region 53
Eastern Bloc 2, 3
EBRD 9, 10, 12, 55-6, 59-60, 68, 98, 99,
    113, 116, 124, 154, 155
  on private investment in central and
    eastern Europe 93
  restructuring funds 94, 120
EC 157
  JOPP (market studies) 124
economic indicators 6
  inadequacy of 147, 158-60
  requirement for new 158-60
  see also macro-economic
    factors; micro-economic factors
economic reform see reform
Economic and Social Research
    Council, UK 58
economists 153
education 150
EEIM (East European Investment
    Magazine) 15, 17, 20, 107, 113
EIU (Economist Intelligence Unit) 12
elections, preparation for 66
Emerging Markets Profiles (Ernst &
    Young) 12, 13
employee leveraged buy-outs 77
energy development 67
environment, attitudes to 149
environmental costs 159
equity finance 124
Ernst & Young 12, 13, 87, 88
Estonia, ranking 23-4
EU 1, 5, 55, 68, 120, 121
  admission of central European
    states to 3
  aluminium imports into from CIS
    155-7 (Table 8.1)
  Association Agreements with
    central European four 122
  and consultants 61-2
  Poland applies to join 15
  protectionism 122, 125-6, 135
  restructuring funds 94, 120
EU PHARE 56, 57, 60, 62, 155
EU TACIS 56, 57, 60, 62, 155
Euromoney 12
Eurostat 159
expectations 7, 134
  closing the gap 126-8

gap 11, 57, 111-12, 153-4
  narrowing the gap 157-8
  of privatisation 82, 83
export credit insurance 124
export promotion 114, 134-6
exporting companies 96

fascism, in Russia 57
feasibility studies 124, 126-7
Fiat 131
fiscal and monetary policy 66, 123
foreign exchange regime 122
foreign investment
  average size 119 (Table 6.4)
  in Belarus 36 (Figure 2.3)
  by country 121 (Table 6.5)
  case studies 128-32
  competitive advantage 117-20
  contributions to reform process
    114-16
  non-capital 114-16
  cumulative committed (1990-93)
    106 (Table 6.1)
  in Czech Republic 17-18 (Figures
    2.2 and 2a)
  direct 2, 17-18
  history of 112
  interaction with privatisation 84-5
  in Kyrgystan 46 (Figure 2.4)
  methods of 108-11 (Figure 6.2)
  methods of
    Czech Republic 110 (Figure 6.2)
    Hungary 109 (Figure 6.2)
    Poland 109 (Figure 6.2)
    Russia 110 (Figure 6.2)
  motivation for 117
  number of enterprises 107
    (Figure 6.1)
  in Poland 14 (Figure 2.1)
  principal inhibitors 120-2
  principal sectors 115-16
    (Table 6.3)
  regional affiliations 120-1
foreign investors
  main concerns of in Poland 139
    (Figure 7.1)
  surveys of 139-48
foreign-owned companies 116
France 59, 120, 156, 157

171

freedom of information and expression 160
FSM (Poland) 129, 131
FSO (Poland) 129, 131
funding sources, technical assistance 55-6 (Table 3.1)

G24 60, 154
G7 10, 55, 57, 59
   funds in Russia 94
Gallup 58
GDP
   foreign investment as a percentage of 114
   inadequacy as indicator 10, 12, 147, 158, 159
   percentage generated from the private sector 85-6 (Table 4.3)
General Electric, investment in Tungsram 20
General Motors 131
Georgia, ranking 53
Germany 120-1
   export credit facility (Hermes) 124
   reunification 4
globalisation 3, 112
GNP 158, 159
Gorbachev, Mikhail 1, 7, 57
Gorky Automobile Works (GAZ), Russia 79-80
government assistance, the effect of 122-4
government departments, restructuring of 67
governments
   attitudes and support for foreign investment 116, 123-4
   and company restructuring 103-4
   and foreign investors 158
   industrial policies 95
   and post-privatisation phase 83-4
   and private sector 157
Great Britain *see* UK
greenfield sites 108-11, 118, 121
Greenspan, Alan 159
Greenwald, Gerald 102

Hahn, Carl 130
Hanson PLC 106, 120

Henderson, Hazel 158
Hermes 124
holistic approach to reform xvi, 152, 153
human development 159
human rights 160
HungarHotels, case study 81-2
Hungarian Law, Transformation Act 81
Hungarians, in Romania, Slovakia and former Yugoslavia 20, 21, 34
Hungary 5, 67, 73, 94, 96, 122, 128
   1994 opinion polls 58
   attitudes 145, 161
   company reconstruction 100-2
   methods of foreign investment 109-110 (Figure 6.2)
   OECD exports 135 (Table 6.7)
   percentage of GDP generated from the private sector 85-6 (Table 4.3)
   privatisation methods 75, 77
   ranking 12, 20-1
   stock market 84, 133, 134

IBM Germany 101
IFC (International Finance Corporation) 94, 99, 124
IMF (International Monetary Fund) 69, 71, 148, 159
   and Bulgaria 27
   consistent approach 7-10
   criticisms of 9-10
   economic conditions xvi
   founded 1944 7
   and Kyrgystan 47
   mandate 8
   role in central Europe 8
   and Russia 32
indicators 9-10, 114; *see also* economic indicators
individual privatisations 73, 76-7, 80
industries, identifying second tier 95
industry
   rebuilding local 92-105
   residual State holdings in 67
inflation 147
infrastructure 9, 123
   attitudes of foreign investors to 139-41 (Figures 7.1-4)

projects 67
Intercomalum 156
international institutions 160
    role of 154
International Paper Co, US 99
investment
    by the West 106-36
    countries for future 143 (Figure 7.7)
investments, case-by-case 94
investor attitudes 160
investor protection legislation 67, 84,
    133
inward investment 67, 96, 115-16
Iran 50
Italy 120

Japan 156, 159
Japanese companies 120
job maintenance 114
joint ventures 2, 77, 108-11, 112, 116,
    118
J P Morgan 99

Kadar 58
Kalbe, Peter 62
Kazakhstan 31, 67
    ranking 29-30
Keynes, John Maynard 8
Klaus, Vaclav 18, 79, 159
know how, transfer of, *see* technology
    transfer
Kyrgystan
    foreign investment in 46 (Figure 2.4)
    ranking 46-7

Latin America 120
Latvia, ranking 25-6
legislation 116, 122
    new 66
legislative stability, attitudes of foreign
    investors to 141 (Figure 7.5)
liberalisation 4, 112
liquidation method 77
Lithuania, ranking 38
Ljunggren, A 99
loans 154
local businesses, resentment of foreign
    investment 111
local economy, status of, in various

countries 13
local governments 67, 69
London Club 15, 27

macro-economic factors 9-10, 66, 114,
    126, 147, 158
management
    competence of 146 (Figure 7.12)
    quality of 95
management buy-outs 77
management skills 114
    shortage of 96
management techniques
    US 149
    western 103, 149
manpower, in various countries 13
market, attitudes of foreign investors
    to local 142 (Figure 7.6)
market economy 11
    variety of models xvi
Marshall Plan, rejected 4, 59-60
Marxism-Leninism 2
mass privatisation 73, 74, 161
    methods 75 (Table 4.2); 78-80
    Poland 59, 79
meat sector, Poland 88-90
medium sized companies 120-1
mentality *see* attitudes
micro-economic factors 126, 147, 160
microwave technology 97
MIGA (Multinational Investment
    Guarantee Agency) 99
Miszertechnika 101
Mitterand, François 7, 10, 130
Modus 58
Moldova (Moldavia) 54
    ranking 53
Monnet, Jean 149
monopoly suppliers 119-20
motivation 146 (Figure 7.11)
multinationals xvi, 27, 116, 120, 121,
    125
Muslim fundamentalism, in
    Uzbekistan 43
mutual funds, closed-end 132

NAFTA (North American Free Trade
    Agreement) 1
National Bank of Hungary 21

national budgeting 68
nationalism xvi, 3, 153
Nazarbaev, President of Kazakhstan 29, 30
negotiations 152
changes in the style of 126-7
Netherlands 120
New Economics school 158-9
niche opportunities 119, 121
Nordic countries 23, 25, 38

objectives of privatisation
external 78
macro-economic 78
micro-economic 78
political 78
OECD 12, 159
exports from central Europe 135 (Table 6.7)
Opel 131
OPIC (Overseas Private Investment Corporation) 99
opinion polls 58, 138, 160
western companies on investment climates 122-4
oral traditions 2

PAP Business News 99
paperless share transaction system 91
Paris Club 15
Perm, prostitutes of 79
personal relationships, in particularist culture 151-2 (Figure 7.14)
PIFS *see* UK Know How Fund
Pilkington 119
PlanEcon 12
Poland 5, 12, 66, 67, 73, 96, 116, 118, 119, 122
1993 elections 135-6
antipathy to USSR 2
attitudes 146, 147-8
automotive sector 131-2
foreign investment in 14 (Figure 2.1)
foreign investment in, methods 109-10 (Figure 6.2)
main concerns of foreign investors 139 (Figure 7.1)
mass privatisation 59, 79
meat sector 88-90

OECD exports 135 (Table 6.7)
percentage of GDP generated from the private sector 85-6 (Table 4.3)
political/economic bridge 58-9
privatisation methods 75, 76, 77
pulp and paper industrial restructuring 99-100
ranking 14-16
role of IMF in 8
sectoral privatisation 92-3
stock market 59, 84, 133, 134
political risk
insurance 99
in various countries 13
political structures 66
politicians 153-4
politics, and technical assistance 57-9
pollution 36
Polonez 131
portfolio investment 132-4
post-privatisation success 82-4, 157
Prague 74
price reform 66
private sector 71-91, 160, 161
percentage of GDP generated from 85-6 (Table 4.3)
private trade associations 111
privatisation 66, 71-91
case studies 86-91
continuing the momentum 82-3
and destination of cash outcomes 123
emphases of various methods 78-80
interaction with foreign investment 84-5
major problems 82-6
mechanistic definition 71
methods 73 (Table 4.1)
objectives 77-8
reasons for 71-3
speed of 6, 118-19
type of 73-7
in UK 72-3
Procter and Gamble 119
profitability, and structure 95
project definition 63-4
property, ownership of 160-1
protectionism 111, 132
EU 122, 125-6, 135

need for less 155-7
public sector reform 66
pulp and paper industrial
    restructuring, Poland 99-100

quality of life 6, 145 (Figure 7.10); 147,
    157, 159, 161
Quintus 81-2

recession (1990s) 4, 7, 112
reform
    externally inspired programmes
        149-50
    holistic approach xvi, 152, 153
    mixed picture of 5-6
    political and social consequences
        153
    positive aspects 160-1
    progress to 12-54, 143
    and technical assistance 55
Registration Place Trading System
    (RMS), Czech Republic 90-1
regulation 66, 133
Renault 130
reporting standards 133
resources, natural 117
restructuring 79, 83, 92-105
    financial 92-4
    industrial 92-4
    main problems 94-6
    percentage of western investors in
        favour of 93 (Table 5.1)
    see also company restructuring
return on capital 106
Reuters 12
risk analyses 148
risk management technique 127-8
Romania 27, 67
    Cluj, Ursus brewery 76, 87-8
    foreign investment 108
    ranking 39-40
Romanian Development Bank 88
Rostelecom 97
Russia 66, 67, 119, 123-4, 129, 135
    1993 elections 6
    1994 local elections 6
    foreign investment 108
    methods of 109 (Figure 6.2)
    G7 funds 94

government at odds with
    parliament 6
outlook on reform 5-6
privatisation methods 75, 77
privatisation programme 6, 79-80
ranking 31-3
role of IMF in 8, 9
telecommunications 96-8
voucher privatisation 58
Russian Central Bank 6, 32
Russian Ministry of
    Telecommunications 97
Russian White House, shelling of 57
Russians, in Latvia 25
Rutherford, Jack 102

Sachs, Jeffrey 8
safety standards 5
St Petersburg auction 79
SAS, model of joint ownership and
    global strategic relationship 5
satellite communications 97
Scandinavians 128
science and technology, in various
    countries 13
secondary markets 82, 84
sectoral privatisation 73, 74-6
    methods 80
sectoral reconstruction 96-100
sectors, foreign investment in 115-16
    (Table 6.3)
share issues 72, 76, 91
share trading mechanisms 74
Shelby, David 102
Single European Market 122
Skoda 129, 130-1, 138
Slovakia 94, 122
    ranking 34-5
    voucher privatisation 74
Slovenia 12
    ranking 22
small and medium sized companies,
    116
    UK, investment in Russia 124
small service businesses 66
small-scale privatisation 73, 77
social assistance 66, 67, 148
social issues 10, 148
socialism 77

socio-economic implications 66
Solidarity 90
South Africa 1
South-east Asia 70
southern Europeans 128
stability 114, 122
of various countries 13
Stalin 95, 119
standard of living 6
star opportunities 119-20
statistical data 66
unreliability of xvii, 137
stock exchanges 67
and portfolio investment 133-4
(Figure 6.3)
stock markets 84, 132-4
structural readjustment problems 161
surveys, of foreign investors 139-48
Sweden 58
Systems of National Accounts 159

Tadzhikistan 53
ranking 52
Tatra 102-3
key performance indicators 103
(Table 5.3)
technical assistance 4, 9, 154, 157
appropriateness and relevance 69
conditionality of 69
content of 55
funding sources 55-6 (Table 3.1)
funds 104
impact of 124-6
phases in model of development 65-
8 (Figure 3.2)
and politics 57-9
reasons for poor success rate 69-70
requirements 65-8
and stability 123
who benefits? 64-5
technology, out-of-date 95
technology transfer 55-70, 114
effectiveness of 60-1
telecommunications 67
comparisons of 140 (Figure 7.2)
Russia 96-8
telephone system, two-tier Russian 97-8
tenders, preparation of 63-4
Thatcher, Margaret 7, 10

time, attitudes to 149
timing, of foreign investment for
competitive advantage 118-19
tourism 27
trade policies 67, 134-6
trading conditions 123
training 150
Trompenaars, Fons 148-52
Turkey 50
Turkmenistan 53, 54
ranking 52

UK 120
Department of Trade and
Industry 123-4
privatisation in 72-3
UK Know How Fund 55, 56, 60, 61, 68,
87, 91
Pre-Investment Feasibility Study
Grant Scheme (PIFS) 124
TIPS (training) 124
Ukraine, ranking 48-9
UN 159
UNDP (United Nations Development
Programme) 158
Human Development Index (HDI)
159
UNECE (United Nations
Economic Commission for
Europe) 12, 14, 17, 18, 107
unemployment 66, 96, 147, 148, 161
as a result of privatisation 84
United States of America *see* US
Ursus brewery, Cluj, Romania 76, 87-8
US 1, 156
companies 120, 121
free trade agreement with Canada 1,
122
investment in Russia 31
US AID 55, 56
US Federal Reserve 159
USSR 1
banking system 4
foreign investment law xv
political effects on trade 4-5
see also CIS
Uzbekistan, ranking 42-3
valuation, asset or business 81
Videoton

Index

case study 100-2
    main performance indicators 101
    (Table 5.2)
Vietnam 112
Visegrad Agreement 5, 122
Volkswagen 130-1, 138
voucher privatisation 72
    Czech Republic 18, 19, 58, 74
    Russia 58
    Slovak 74

wage controls 148
Warsaw Bourse 84
West, investment by the 106-36
western Europe 7, 120, 121, 122
work attitudes, attitudes of foreign
    investors to 143-6 (Figures 7.8-12)
work ethic 145-6
workshops 127

specialist facilitation skills 127
World Bank 10, 27, 47, 55, 56, 68-9, 71,
    120, 159
world capitalism 7
World Economic Forum 139-42, 145-6
    World Link 12, 13
world institution, new 10-11
world institutions, pressures on 1
World Link (World Economic Forum)
    12, 13
world market prices 4

Yeltsin, Boris 9, 32, 57, 79
Yugoslavia 2, 154
    war in 27, 41

Zaklady Celulozowo Papiernicze S.A.
    (Kwidzyn mill) 99